Confessions of a GIRL

Truth to be Told

by
TESSA SEAN HERSHBERGER

Fresh Writers Books
13386 Judy Ave NW, Uniontown OH 44685

Confessions of a Girl
Copyright © 2005 Tessa Hershberger
All rights reserved. No part of this book may be reproduced or transmitted in any form or by any means, electronic or mechanical, including photocopying, recording, or by any information or storage retrieval system without written permission from the publisher.

Author: Tessa Hershberger

Publisher: Bill Jelen

Acquisitions Editor: Rick Friedline

Project Manager: Catherine Schoenewald

Editor: Paragon Prepress, Inc.

Cover Illustration: Megan Hawranick

Cover Design: Shannon Mattiza

Author Photo: Dallas Wallace, Paramount Photo

Prepress: Paragon Prepress, Inc.

Marketing Team: Jessica Baker, Brittany Brasill, Kellen Burkholder, Jennifer Burns, Lindsey Cotton, Phillip Croft, Jacquelyn Dorsey, Brianna Fox, Briana Gergon, Britney Justice, Cory Kocher, Brittani McCutcheon, Abby Miller, Erin Nabors, Ashley Naso, Ross Nisly, Adam Pearce, Jeremy Roberts, Brooke Sanner, Kaitlyn Schumacher, Tyler Sutton, Danielle Wood, Advisor: Suzanne Arnold.

Published by: Fresh Writers Books, 13386 Judy Ave NW, Uniontown OH 44685
Distributed by: Independent Publishers Group
First Printing: March 2005. Printed in India
Library of Congress Control Number: 2004113921
ISBN: 1-932802-97-5

Contents

About the Author		v
Acknowledgments		vi
Dedication		viii
Introduction		1
1	My Generation: Right Where I'm supposed to be	5
2.	A Predetermined Mission: The Chance to Make History	17
3.	What's Love got to do with it? A Lot!	35
4.	Where Moth and Rust Destroy: Where are Your Treasures?	79
5.	Who's That in the Mirror? The False Image We've Formed	107
6.	Looking Through the Father's Eyes: The Truth to Who We Are	135
7.	Modesty: A New Approach	157
8.	It's all in the Mind: God's Greater Calling to Purity on the Inside	169
9.	A Hope and a Future: Learning to Trust God with the Puzzle of Life	189
10.	Finishing the Race: Keeping the Bar Raised and the Passion Strong	209

About the Author

Tessa Sean Hershberger is a high school senior. From the outside, she has been the typical, involved, "A+" student. Her many extracurricular activities have included French Club, Junior Class Treasurer, Fellowship of Christian Athletes, National Honors Society, and leader of the Sign Language Club. That is what is seen from the outside.

On the inside, she's quietly been observing the ways of her peers day in and day out and slowly realizing the hope that so many girls living in this generation need to hear. Spending nine years in a private Christian school and then spending four more in a public high school, she has known girls from all different backgrounds and has come to discover a central thing that she believes to be missing in so many girls that are living in her generation- something that God has been revealing to her for the past year and a half, something that she is working hard to possess, and something that she truly longs to encourage her peers to possess along with her.

She was once very in tune with her culture, possessing some of its very same values and morals, and yet she has found a different path that she is excitedly choosing to follow. And one of her biggest passions in life is to invite all young women and girls to join her in this adventurous life.

Tessa was a winner in the 2004 Fresh Writers Writing Program. This program encourages high school students to consider literary careers and funds a summer co-op program during which this book was created. For more information about the Fresh Writers program, **contact Bill@FreshWritersBooks.com**

Acknowledgments

Who do I thank first for one of the most amazing opportunities of my life? I want to start off by thanking my parents, Joe and Gayle Hershberger, because without you I would not be the person I am today. Your unconditional love and support has blessed me over and over again. I love you both so much. Second, I want to thank my sisters Abby and Carly- you both have taught me a lot about myself and I thank you for that- I love you! Thank you from the bottom of my heart to all of my amazing friends out there- Jillian Amann, Allison Hupp, Jonathan Thurman, Zach Harig, Leah Dillworth, Heidi Hershberger, Colleen Mueller, Ryan Wells, Julie Cooper, Maria Nisly, CayeDee Rhoades, Kayla Detwiler, Lauren Hopkins (and all you other set-aparts, you know who you are!), Julie Myers, Chris Lowe, Ashley Vandegrift, Hannah Abdul, Kathryn Foust, and whoever else I am leaving out (forgive me!) You have all been an inspiration to me in one way or another and you all hold a special place in my heart. Thank you Megan Hawranick for the awesome cover design- you are so talented! Thank you to all of my past English teachers who encouraged me to keep writing- you've truly made a difference in my life. Thank you to the wonderful role models I have had in the past few years that have supported me and encouraged me to go deeper in my relationship with God- Renee Nisly, Christa Domer, Sandy Amann, Sherri Landis, Cathy Calvelli, Eric and Leslie Ludy, Chad and June Miller, Walt and Mary Louise Raber, Pastor Henry Shrock, Pastor Dave Hall and Pam Moore. Thank you to my fellow young authors Ashley Henneman-you've been an amazing friend to me!- Josh Moorhead, and Lee Galada. I'm so glad I could share this experience with you guys! THANK YOU to the person that made my dream a reality, Bill Jelen. How can I thank you enough for your patience, encouragement, and the many hours that you put in to this? I will never be able to repay you for your kindness! Lastly, the most important thank you goes to my Savior, my Best Friend, my Hope, my Joy, and my Peace- Jesus Christ. You have been an overflowing blessing in my life and I want to give everything back to You. Thank You for being the Author of my story. I love You.

Dedication

I want to dedicate this book first to my loving Jesus who gave me the passion to put my thoughts down on paper and share them with the world. Second, I want to dedicate this book to my family and friends who have been the most amazing people in my life over and over. Thirdly, I want to dedicate this book to my generation- every young person out that is searching for the truth, desires to find something more, and longs for eternal fulfillment. This book is written for you.

Introduction:

It's Only Me Talking

Before I started writing this book, I thought for a while about how I wanted it to sound. After all, at the time I'm writing this, I'm only seventeen. Will people really take me seriously? Well, I guess I'm about to find out. I didn't want to come off as sounding like a snobby know-it-all who thinks she has all the answers in life, yet I didn't want to undermine my opinion and timidly mumble a bunch of thoughts that would be left for you to interpret in a hundred different ways. All I really wanted to do was be honest and to take what was in my heart and put it into words. As I'm writing, I'm not only writing to my generation (and anyone else who wants to listen), but I'm also writing to myself. The issues I'm going to write about in this book are issues that I'm going through every day. I don't want to write about something that I *haven't* gone through because I want this book to be coming from experience, and most of all from my heart. I'm by no means trying to sound better than anyone else who's reading this book and I'm not writing this book to say, "Look at what I'm doing. You should do it too!" I'm writing it to say, "This is what I'm going through, this is how God is speaking to me, and this is how I think our generation can make a huge difference in the world." I don't know what you'll get out of this book but my prayer is that God will speak to your heart and that you'll be inspired to take on a stronger walk with Him. I hope you'll find what I have to say an encouragement and that you'll relate to at least one of the things I have to say. If, in the end, when you've finished reading the book, you find yourself with a greater passion for God's purpose for your life, then my mission will have been accomplished. I'm praying for you as you read this and I want you to know that God is waiting to do something huge in your life. You were created for *such a time as this*. Your days were thought out long before you were born and God purposely put you on Earth for this very hour. God has been chasing after your heart since the day you were born and more than anything His desire is for you to give it totally and completely to Him. I'm inviting you, and God's inviting you, to come. Come with a broken spirit and lay your life before the cross. Come before your generation and inspire it to live a life of new purpose that only God could dream up. The moment you lay it all down, God will pull you up and transform you into the exquisite child of God that you were born to be. Come.

Praying for you,

Tessa Sean Hershberger
June 2004

P.S. Throughout the book I have included spaces for you to write your own thoughts about the topics: how you feel about them, how they relate to you, what you think God is telling you about them, and things you disagree with and agree with. You can even use them as places to write prayers to God. There are also some spaces that give you specific things to write about. I encourage you to not leave them blank and skip over them, but fill them up with your own words like you were writing in a journal. You'll be thankful to have so many thoughts down on paper that you can go back and refer to later on.

Chapter 1

My Generation: Right Where I'm Supposed To Be

WHO AM I?

My generation intrigues me to the bones. I've fallen in love with quietly observing the different personalities, the different ideas, the different fashions, the different passions, and the different ways of getting the heads of the opposite sex turn, stare, and then run into a pole only to embarrass the living hormones out of them. I am living in an extremely unique generation and though I can't say I'm enjoying every minute of it, I can say that I know I'm exactly where I'm supposed to be.

Exactly what generation am I in? Well, I'm 17 and I was born in 1986. Until now, I've always thought I was in what people refer to as "Generation X." I kind of like the term actually. When I hear it I think of words like "EXcellent, EXciting, EXtraordinary…and EXtreme. But I wanted to get my facts straight so I got on the Internet to see just who Generation X consists of. I ended up finding several different opinions on when Generation X stopped, and to my surprise the date was always around the late 1970s or the very early 1980s. In the Miriam Webster dictionary it says that Generation X is "A group of people born between 1961 and 1972 typified by a college education, dissatisfaction with career opportunities, and pessimism." So, Webster basically says my mom is in Generation X but I'm not, nor were any of my babysitters. Okay. I then found out that the next generation after Generation X is called the millennial generation. So, am I a GenXer or a millennial baby? I'm not exactly sure because it seems as though the term "Generation X" is always used in such a broad way to describe teenagers and for the record, I've only heard the word "millennial" once in my life (actually, I've never even heard the word, I've only read it...one time... and the definition for it wasn't even in the 1999 edition of Webster's Dictionary).

Maybe people just throw around the term "Generation X" without really knowing what it means or maybe I was always just confused about the term myself. So honestly, I guess I'm a millennial kid.

I don't really think it matters whether or not you know the real term of what generation you're in, but just to get an idea of where you stand compared to someone my age, see how many of these questions you can (honestly) answer "yes" to.

1. Can you name the six main characters on *Saved by the Bell?*

2. Do you (or did you at one time) own one of the following debut CDs?
    a) Hanson
    b) Amy Grant
    c) New Kids on the Block

d) Backstreet Boys
   e) N'SYNC
   f) Michael W. Smith

3. Did you see *Titanic* in theatres more than once?

4. Does your cell phone ring to Mandy Moore's latest song?

5. Have you ever owned one or more of the following?
   a. My Little Pony
   b. Beanie Babies
   c. Nintendo
   d. Light Bright
   e. Easy Bake Oven
   f. Furbie (those always freaked me out big time)

6. Did you ever wear stir-up pants, a flannel shirt, and a humongous scrunchie all at the same time?

7. Have you ever worn your hair in a huge side ponytail?

8. Would you recognize O.J. Simpson walking down your street?

9. Can you name the cast of *Friends* in five seconds or less? (OK, so I've never even watched a whole episode of *Friends*!)

10. Did you ever own anything in bright neon colors?

If you answered "yes" to most of these questions, you'll probably relate to my voice pretty well in this book. But honestly, your grandma might be able to answer "yes" to all these questions too, so really this doesn't prove anything. I just wanted to see if you could remember that the Backstreet Boys were cool once. I forgot.

CONFESSIONS OF A GIRL

Now that we have that covered, I'm going to stop using all the technical terms and just refer to my generation as "my generation" so no one gets confused. And who am I speaking to in my generation? Every young woman and girl that's willing to listen. (And any guy that's somewhat curious.) Whether you want to call me a GenXer or a millennial baby, I don't care. All I can say is that my generation is the generation I was born for. There's *so* much to say about it. It's one of a kind and though sometimes I wish I could go back to the '20s and get a bob or the '50s and wear saddle shoes, I'd have to say that in the end I'd rather be here. (Anyways, I had a pair of saddle shoes in Kindergarten.) There's so much that has happened in history during my lifetime that involves my peers and there are so many different personalities out there. I know I belong here.

I have lived in my generation for 17 years. I have a heart completely full of inspiration and for a while now it's been dying to be heard. *This is me! This is what I have to say! This is how I feel, this is what I think, and this is what I want the rest of the world to know. Come over here and join me while I bask in the Truth that I have discovered.*

- - -

IN THE MIDST OF IT ALL
This what my generation is telling me…in the midst of the Truth I've found

I say I belong in my generation, not because I fit in, but I actually say it because I stand out like a Prada pumping Paris Hilton on the set of Survivor. *Look, here I am! I've discovered something different that I think you'll want to hear. A unique way of thinking. Something fresh. Something you might only hear from me. Or…wait! Do I only wish I stood out in my generation that much? Is it only a fantasy of mine to have*

MY GENERATION: RIGHT WHERE I'M SUPPOSED TO BE

not turned my back from this one-of-a-kind Truth too many times and packed my suitcase to travel the overgrown road of mindless conformity?

Some days I decide that I've had enough of the lies and deception that are thrown at me and that I'll no longer listen to the twisted values and morals that my generation is telling me are "right" and "accepted" and "normal." Then the next day I'm stuffing my face with fruit to get that must-have "healthy glow" that I read about in last month's issue of some popular fashion magazine. The next thing you know I'm pounding my head on the wall after finding out that one slice of watermelon has a gut popping 150 calories. (And for the record…I did just find out that one slice of watermelon has 150 calories. I hope that's a pretty big slice because I'll never skimp out on watermelon.)

Everything around me seems so unstable. Why can't I just decide to believe one single thing and then base everything I do off of that truth? Instead, I feel like I'm going up and down, up and down, as if I'm on a teeter-totter, only it's not as innocent as a child on a playground but it's as serious as a seventeen-year-old trying to figure out life and the total truth of it all. The thing is, I feel as though I *have* figured out the total truth of it all. It's only a matter of living that truth out and abandoning the ways of my generation to follow after that truth, no matter what the price is, every single day of my life.

Abandon the ways of your generation? Is this some kind of joke? No, I'm sorry, it's not. It's real, it's possible, and it's basically what the rest of the book is about so if you're not too sure about the whole idea, go ahead, put it down. But for those of you who are the least bit curious about what I have to say, read on.

— — —

1 Corinthians 3:18-19, "Do not deceive yourselves. If any one of you thinks he is wise by the standards of this age, he should become a "fool" so that he may become wise. For the wisdom of this world is foolishness in God's sight. As it is written: 'He catches the wise in their craftiness'." (NIV)

The ways of my generation. What exactly are they? Like I said before, my generation is very unique. Not only are we unique, we're what I would like to call "complicated" and perhaps somewhat looked down upon by the older generations. We've been beat down until we're left with a crummy image of ourselves that we're not sure what to do with. I feel as though a large part of the older generations looks at my generation with a frown, a frown of disappointment. It's like they're saying…*so this is what we get next? These are the kids that are going to step up and take over the nation? This country is surely set for doom. I've got to get out of here.*

It's really a shame that they've placed us in such a fixed persona; one that I think will be very hard to escape from. We aren't *that* bad, are we? I've heard countless stories of people in my age group branching out and making a difference in the world. I've heard accounts of ordinary teens that have done huge things just because their hearts were in the right places. I've read dozens of articles about young people going on mission trips, raising money for the poor, helping the elderly, doing random acts of kindness, and so on. So what's the problem with us? Why can't we seem to get it right in the eyes of authority?

And then I hear a faint voice. *It's the fact that your generation has picked the wrong "authority" altogether. It's the fact that the authority you have chosen is false. It's telling you lie after lie, setting trap after trap waiting for the day when you'll stick your foot in the mud and die trying to get it out.*

MY GENERATION: RIGHT WHERE I'M SUPPOSED TO BE

You've chosen to follow an authority that is giving you a false truth, a false hope, a false self-image, and a false perception of what life is really about. You've walked out on anything real and you're giving yourselves up to a scam.

So where is this false truth coming from? It's coming from the million branches of the media, it's coming from politicians, it's coming from (some) of our parents, and unfortunately, it's even coming from our closest friends. To put it in a nutshell, the false truth is coming from a little something I like to call *society*. Our society has set a number of standards for America's youth to live up to and they're rock solid. It's practically a matter of life and death to escape from the way they've molded themselves into our culture.

Society has first set the standard for money and possessions. *Money is everything, and unless you've got a lot of it, well, good luck in life.* We've been given the directive that we *have* to buy everything we can afford or else we're poor nobodies without any worth. Our financial status will make us or break us. We must do everything we can to keep ourselves from becoming a "have-not." *Risk your life to join the "haves."* So this message plays over and over in our minds, like a broken record that plays the same melody over and over and over. The standard was set a long time ago and it has slowly become accepted.

A second standard that society has set is the standard of relationships. It has shown us that divorce is now a normal, everyday part of life. It happens. Don't shoot for a lifelong partner because you'll be lucky to make it to your 10th anniversary. Love? What is love anymore? Bang. That's just it. We don't even know. We can't even tell you what the real thing is. How can we tell when most of our examples of relationships are artificial failures? How can we tell when magazines tell us twenty different things? *Twenty reasons why it's more fun to be single! How to turn your friend into your boyfriend! Go from crush to love!* You're right. We can't tell.

Thirdly, society has set a standard for how we should look. Just *how many* fashion and beauty magazines out there are directed towards young women and girls? And it's not even just girls. Guys have been given the standard just as much. If we don't look a certain way, dress in certain clothes, and say the right things, we're just not doing it right. *You need a makeover and you need it* now!! I don't know about you but that's the message that I'm getting. My hair is not the right color. My arms are *too* flabby. I'm *not* on the right diet. I'm wearing the *wrong* brand name. Again. And I find myself believing it all, because society has wrapped it up in a harmless looking gift box. Needless to say, I opened it up. It was empty.

Society has not only set a standard for wealth, relationships, and appearance, but it has also set a standard for behavior. There's a certain way for guys to act, and there's a certain way for girls to act. *Guys: Act tough or go home. Don't show your emotions. Just get the girl and get on with it. Stay cool. "Keep it real" (whatever that means). Girls: Be sexy, but don't let the guy use you. Take control over the relationship. Be strong. Don't let the guy get the better of you. Hold it in. Don't cry. Move on. Get out there and show yourself.*

We hear it over and over again. And now it has stuck. It has stuck like glue, and I've believed it one too many times. It's affected me so much that I've felt stupid for not flirting before. It's affected the decisions I've made when buying my clothes. As hard as I've tried to escape it, there's no telling that it hasn't affected me. It has. And it's affected my generation as well.

Yes, society has told us many things; things that are extremely easy to believe, even if you think you're smart enough not to. Society has ultimately become our authority figure and whether it is friends, the media, or your high school English teacher, society has surrounded us like water surrounds an island. It has become a part of how we stay afloat in life. It "supports" us and "comforts" us. It answers us when we question life. But let me tell you- a large part of society is only waiting for us to sink, waiting for our hearts to become so heavy that life isn't even an option. We're holding on, and it's just waiting for the perfect moment to blind our eyes for the very last time and convince us to let go. And let's face it: it isn't waiting to catch us after the fall.

My Own Thought
What standard that society has set has affected you the most and why? How do you feel about that standard? Is it true? Is it easy to live up to?

_____

_____

_____

_____

_____

A SINGLE PROPOSITION

Now would be the time to pay attention
Acts 2:40, "…he warned them; and he pleaded with them, 'Save yourselves from this corrupt generation'." (NIV)

I hesitantly take baby steps to center stage. The spotlight is shining in my eyes and I step up to the microphone. The audience is impatiently waiting for me to begin speaking. I nervously shuffle my feet as my brow sweats and my hands become jelly. I tap the microphone to make sure it's on and a loud, screeching ring of feedback immediately sends the audience into an annoyed frenzy of groans. My heart jumps and I suddenly wish that the floor would open up and swallow me. *No. You have to say this. Get back up there and say it with confidence.* They might laugh. *It doesn't matter.* They'll think I'm crazy! *It's a possibility.* But if I don't say it now...*you'll regret it*...I'll regret it.

So, here goes. I have a single proposal to my generation. I have a *plea to* my generation. So, if you're interested, listen up. **Let's raise the bar. Let's run away in reckless abandonment of the world. Let's dance in the Truth. Let's live the lives we are being called to. Let's set the standard higher than it's ever been before. Our generation was born for *such a time as this.***

I feel very strongly that our generation can do better, that we can prove society wrong and begin to climb the ladder to the one and only Truth. Our generation has so much to offer to the world and it's about time that we stepped in and made a worldwide, permanent change. God has called us on a mission and we must take the responsibility to answer that call.

My Thoughts

_____

_____

_____

_____

_____

MY GENERATION: RIGHT WHERE I'M SUPPOSED TO BE

Chapter 2

A Predetermined Mission: The Chance to Make History

A ONCE IN A LIFETIME OPPORTUNITY
One that I just can't seem to pass up!

1 Timothy 4:12, "Don't let anyone look down on you because you are young, but set an example for the believers in speech, in life, in love, in faith, and in purity." (NIV)

A few months ago I started taking an interest in reading the newspaper every day (or at least bits and pieces). It all started when I discovered a daily column in my newspaper, *The Akron Beacon Journal*, called *Porter's People*. It's a small column that has a bunch of tidbits of gossip here and there that mostly deal with stupid things people do or say. They're mostly about celebrities, and then there's one of my favorite tidbits entitled "Dumb Crook News" which always offers a laugh. And there's always one entitled "The Final Word" that usually comes from a latenight television host and makes fun of some highly targeted politician.

CONFESSIONS OF A GIRL

In today's paper I found out the following: Janet Jackson and Justin Timberlake supposedly had some kind of "relationship," which can basically be defined any way you want in Hollywood. Some call it the "55 hour" (speaking of Britney, did you know she just got a new tattoo? I found that out today, too), some call it a "Bennifer," but I guess I just prefer to call it a "Hollywood fling," because, well, flings don't ever last long. Anyways, the column has given me tons of intellectual insight into just how messed up some people in this world are. (Of course I'm very aware that many of the things I read could just be rumors...)

Anyways, after a few weeks of picking up the front page, reading *Porter's People*, and then walking away, I got the urge to read more. I started with the front page (that's usually where the most interesting stories are). As I started to read more and more, or even just glance at the headlines, I soon realized that, *wow*, there are so many bad things going on, things in the world, things in the country, and things particularly with people in my generation. I read about how two guys my age were "harmlessly" messing around and one boy shot the other dead. I've read about young, single mothers starving their babies to death, leaving them to die without telling anyone. I've read about theft, I've read about rape, I've read about sexual harassment, and I've read about pornography. There's nothing bad that *isn't* happening. It seems impossible even to think up the worst situation you can and not read about it in the paper the next week.

It scares me to think that *I and my peers* will soon have to grow up and take charge of such an out-of-control world. Just reading the newspaper has totally opened up my eyes and has exposed them to a world that I didn't want to believe existed. And where do I find myself and my generation? Right in the middle of it all. We're too old to go on in innocent lives of childhood, pretending we don't notice the direction the world is headed, yet we're not old enough to say, "Well, it's too late to do anything now." We're at the exact point in our lives where if we stand around and do nothing for one more second, we're only denying the very essence of who we are, and the indisputable fact that life, whether we like it or not, is going to go on, and it's going to go on fast. No matter *how* hard we fight, no matter *how* many times we try to tell ourselves it's not happening, and no matter *how* many years we live in our parents' house so our moms can still do our laundry and cook us dinner, we are on the brink of becoming the leaders of our nation. With that in mind, we have two choices. We can pretend we don't grasp any part of this concept and go on living our lives as though I never mentioned anything. Or, we can wake up from our sleep, do a little (or a lot) of tweaking here and there, and make huge history.

If we choose the former, I'm afraid that our nation and our world will continue to fall farther and farther away from the truth and will carry on to dig it's own grave, which seems to be getting deeper and deeper every time I turn on the news, and every time I walk through the halls on my way to class. Who knows what state the world will be in by the time our own children grow up? There are absolutely no promises.

However, if we chose the latter of the two choices, and chose to really follow it with our whole hearts, I think the world would do a major one-eighty and cause heads to turn and say, "What's going on? Where did *this* generation come from?" Hearts would soon be full of hope. Pain would, thankfully, not completely dissolve, but remain present in some form, and instead of causing us to sink deeper and stray farther from the truth, would only be seen as an opportunity to grow.

Obviously, my hope is that my generation would choose Plan B. And in all confidence, I don't think my wish has to prove in vain. I don't think it's impossible to step in and be a lifeboat for a sinking world. I truly believe that God has called my generation to something higher. I believe that for some time now He's been quietly whispering in our ears, **"Raise the bar, raise the bar, raise the bar."** We just have to take the time to listen. Well, I'm sorry, but that time is *now*. There's absolutely no more time to waste, no more time to delay.

RAISING THE WHAT?

So, what exactly do I mean by "raising the bar?" I'm sure you've heard the term before, maybe from a coach or a teacher. I actually heard it first from my 8th grade Bible teacher. Time and time again he would encourage my class in our relationships with God and our daily lifestyles, "Raise the bar, raise it higher, raise it higher."

So where does the term "raise the bar" come from anyways? (My mom had to tell me the answer to this one. Until then I thought my teacher had just made it up himself.)

Think of someone who does pole-vaulting and the bar that they're jumping over. Each time that bar is raised, that person has to work harder to reach that bar and get over it. Each time that bar is raised, it's like that athlete is saying, "push me harder, I want to accomplish more, I want to do better, I want to achieve higher things."

At a standard and easily accomplished height, the bar could be compared to the "norm," the "standard,' the "acceptable," the "average" in society. My Bible teacher was telling us to *raise* it. What did he mean? He meant that we don't have to (and shouldn't) settle for what this world is offering us. He was warning us that we shouldn't get comfortable in a world that *should* make us feel like aliens. He wanted us to put our entire hearts into seeking after God, and in the meantime find out that a whole other life was awaiting us. He wanted us to set the example for those following after us and change the way we lived our "ordinary," "typical" lives. *Set a new record for the rest of your world.*

I'm positive that my Bible teacher wasn't asking us too difficult a task to accomplish–that year and the rest of our lives. It was only a matter of whether we were willing to work hard enough.

In *The Message* (an awesome version of the Bible written by Eugene Peterson), 1 Timothy 4:12 says this: "And don't let anyone look down on you because you're young. Teach believers with your life…"

God never said that it was all up to adults to be the example, but He specifically commanded our age group: "Teach believers with your life." God obviously has a lot of confidence in us to be a meaningful example of His truth to the rest of the world or else He wouldn't have bothered to tell us how He felt on this issue. The Bible says, "For Jesus doesn't change – yesterday, today, tomorrow, he's always totally himself." (Hebrews 13:8, Msg) God still thinks the exact same way that He did two thousand years ago. The very same confidence that God had in young people back when David was fighting Goliath is the very same confidence that God has in young people today. God did not one day look down on our generation, frown in disappointment, and give up. God has all the hope in the *universe* for us and He's standing in Heaven cheering us on. He doesn't care that half of us aren't old enough to vote yet. He doesn't care that we're still doing homework every night. He doesn't care that we basically run the fast food industry making minimum wage.

He looks past the position that the world puts us in and holds steadfast to the position that *He* has put us in.

God has placed what I like to call a "beautiful burden" on our generation. The phrase definitely sounds like an oxymoron. When we think of the word burden, words like "heavy load," "problem" and "trouble" come to mind. So how can something as depressing as a burden be beautiful? Well, you have to look at the meaning of burden differently.

Once again I turned to Mr. Webster to see how he defined the word "burden." I found a few different definitions: 1) something carried 2) something difficult to bear emotionally or physically 3) a responsibility; a duty.

I like them all actually. Our beautiful burden *is* something we carry. We've carried it with us in life since we were born and now it's time to take it down off our shoulders and take care of it. What's going to happen when we do that? It's going to turn into definition number two. I never said that my proposal would be easy. It *will* be difficult to bear for a period, and it will take more *spiritual* strength than any other type of strength. But once again, what is our beautiful burden? (See definition 3). That's right. It's a responsibility, a duty, and a *mission*. A *predetermined mission* that God had laid out for us even before He created the world.

How then, is this burden beautiful? Well, the very fact that God is calling us to *carry* this burden is beautiful! Yes, in the midst of an ugly, damaged world, God has placed something beautiful in our hands. The reason it's so beautiful is because it comes from God, and *nothing* in this world is more beautiful than the very character of God Himself. It's pretty amazing to think that the Creator of the Universe has something planned for our very generation. And the awesome thing is that God has not only chosen a "select few" to be a part of this revolutionary movement. If you thought you were going to get out the easy way because you didn't think you were "good enough," I'm sorry, you're wrong. If you thought maybe I was only talking to those who have some kind of "spiritual perfection," then in reality I wouldn't have anyone to be talking to. No one, absolutely no one, besides Christ Himself, possesses any kind of spiritual perfection. And that's exactly why we have no excuse at all to ignore God's calling for us to raise the bar. After we've accepted Jesus into our lives by confessing our sin, asked for forgiveness for our sinful ways, and declared Him the Lord of our life, there is not a criterion we have to meet before God can begin to use us. He simply doesn't think that way. The very moment that we ask Him into our hearts is the very moment that He wants to start using us for His glorious plan. And to Him, that moment couldn't come soon enough.

My Thoughts

_____

_____

_____

_____

_____

_____

_____

Steps towards Unloading the Burden
Changing the World
Author Unknown, <u>Aspiring to Greatness</u>

When I was a young man, I wanted to change the world. I found it was difficult to change the world, so I tried to change my nation. When I found I couldn't change the nation, I began to focus on my town. I couldn't change the town and as an older man, I tried to change my family. Now, as an old man, I realize the only thing I can change is myself, and suddenly I realize that if long ago I had changed myself, I could have made an impact on my family. My family and I could have made an impact on our town. Their impact could have changed the nation and I could indeed have changed the world.

This little story has a huge point that I think is well worth paying attention to. If we are really serious about making a change, if we are really willing to put our whole hearts and minds into changing the world, then we have to make it start with us. I can assure you that nothing is going to happen overnight. Something so huge takes time, patience, willpower, and…baby steps. It *is* difficult to change the world, and it's almost just as difficult to change a nation, let alone even a small town. That is why it can only start with changing ourselves. For now, we can't exactly control whether or not the United States is at war. We can't control who becomes the next President of the United States. We can't control the decisions that are made in the Supreme Court. But right now – I don't care if you're 13 or 73 – we *can* begin to change ourselves. And the more we put in to becoming a generation that seeks after God, the more our town, our nation, and our world will begin to transform.

A PREDETERMINED MISSION: THE CHANCE TO MAKE HISTORY

If you're about to put the book down because you already gave up on yourself three years ago (or last week even), don't. It's never too late to change and *no one's* life is too hard for God to turn around. There's not one heart out there that's too hard for God to soften, and there's not one life that's too far into the deep end that God isn't willing to rescue. It doesn't matter how many mistakes you've made. It doesn't matter how many times you have turned your back on God. It doesn't matter how many miles you've traveled in the wrong direction. God is still there, quietly waiting for you to take the first step. He isn't going to force you or push you around until you finally give in. He wants you to make the decision yourself and as soon as you say two small words, He'll immediately step in and begin to guide your first steps.

What are the two words? *"Yes, God."* Saying yes to God is the first and foremost step we have to take before God can begin His work in us. I think so many times we offer God a "next week maybe," "after high school," or "wait until Sunday during church." But the truth of the matter is we have to say "yes" *now*. And we have to keep saying it every second of every day. God isn't into a "sometimes" decision. He says, "Follow me or don't follow me." Revelation 3:15 says, "…you are neither cold nor hot. I wish you were either one or the other!" (NIV) God wants us to make a choice and stay true to that choice for the rest of our lives.

Unfortunately, we're only humans. We're still going to make mistakes because, even after God has cleansed us of our sin and has taken control over our lives, our human nature will continue to cause us to fall. That's why it's so imperative that we are constantly placing our lives into the hands of the Father and surrendering to His Truth.

- - -

NOT TOMORROW…NOT NEXT YEAR…TODAY

Hebrews 2:3a, "How shall we escape if we ignore such a great salvation?" (NIV)

Have you taken that first step to say yes to God? Have you made Him Lord over your life? Hebrews 3:7 says, "'…today if you hear His voice, do not harden your hearts…'" Do you hear God's voice calling you? Can you feel Him tugging at your heart? Don't let your heart be hard towards His voice any longer! God's ultimate purpose for every single person He created is to come to Him and accept Him as their personal savior. God created you out of the dust of the earth and God is calling you *today* to turn your face towards heaven and accept Him into your life.

Last week I was at a funeral for my mom's uncle, Arthur (we always just referred to him as Uncle Art). I didn't know him very well, but I was pretty sure that he was never a Christian because not many of my relatives on my mom's side are. He had spent his last months in a nursing home as his mind slowly began to fail him due to his old age of a robust 92. As the preacher began his message I thought to myself: *what do you say at a funeral of a person who wasn't a Christian? How do you comfort a mourning crowd when you know the person who passed away isn't in heaven rejoicing at the foot of God's throne because they never made the personal choice to follow Him?* The preacher went on to say that it was a day of celebration because we knew that Uncle Art was walking on golden streets with Jesus. I second-guessed what the preacher said. *Is he only saying that to bring some relief? Is Uncle Art in reality crying out in a fiery pit of scorching heat at this very moment?* To my great surprise, he wasn't. The preacher wasn't glazing over the truth and Uncle Art wasn't suffering. The preacher went on to tell the small gathering of people that in the last six months that Uncle Art was alive, some family members had shared God's awesome message of salvation with him and he had accepted Christ into his life. A tingly feeling went up my spine and a tear almost dropped down my cheek. *God is so awesome!*

Now I know you may start to tell yourself: *So the point of the story is that I can party hard 'till I'm 92 and then quickly ask God into my life before I die so that I'll end up in Heaven. So I don't* really *need God today.* No, that's not the point of the story at all. I wish Uncle Art could have experienced God's salvation 85 years ago. His life would have been a million times more fulfilling and there's no telling how God could have used him for His glorious purpose. The point I want to get across comes in what the preacher went on to say.

His message was that we need God and we need God *now*. We simply cannot wait another moment to ask God to take control of our lives. You always hear the cliché, "Live as though today was your last day on Earth." We hear it and we think to ourselves: *OK, I've got to be nicer to so-and-so today. I'm going to take more risks today. I'm not going to let any opportunities pass me by.* It's a good saying to live by, but if we truly understood the depth of the whole saying, and if we truly understood what tomorrow could bring us, we would simply lift our heads from our pillows and vow to ourselves: *Today I am going to make Jesus Christ the Lord of my life. Today I am going to surrender to His will. Today I am going to walk in His truth. Today I am going to choose to follow the narrow road. Because* today *could be my very last chance.*

And it's so true. Today could very well be your last day. Have you made the first step of the rest of your life?

God made it clear in His word that He is *the* only way. The only way to heaven, and the only way in life, period. John 14:6 says, "Jesus answered, 'I am the way and the truth and the life. No one comes to the Father except through me'." (NIV) The first step to life? The first step to changing the world? *Acknowledging that Jesus Christ is the one and only Way and asking Him into your life. Confessing your sins and asking for the forgiveness and redemption that comes only through the cross on which Jesus died to save our very souls.*

If you are ready to begin the greatest journey of your life, come now and lay your life down and with a sincere heart offer this prayer up to God:

Lord, I've been living in the dark and my heart's desire is to come into the light of Your presence. I want to accept into my heart Your beautiful and free gift of grace. I know that I'm a sinner and I ask You to forgive me of the sin that has been ruling in my life. Thank You for your perfect redemption that saved the world when You died on the cross for my sins. Jesus, I want You to become Lord over every single second that I spend on this earth. I want to fulfill the plan that You have for my life and at the end of my days I want to see You in Heaven. I surrender to Your will. Take my life, Lord, and use it. I am Yours.

If you just prayed this prayer and truly meant it, congratulations! You are now a part of the family of God and you have just prayed the most important prayer of your life. It's no longer a matter of life and death, but only a matter of life. Eternal life in heaven awaits you!

Maybe you have already accepted Christ into your heart at an earlier time in your life but you've been wandering in various directions away from the Truth that once ruled over everything you did. Maybe you felt like your relationship with God was getting dry and stationary and that God just somehow forgot about you. Maybe you went through a hard

A PREDETERMINED MISSION: THE CHANCE TO MAKE HISTORY

time in your life that didn't go the way you wanted and you took your eyes off of God's bigger story and attempted to meddle around in what you thought was the rest of your life. There are so many different reasons why we could have strayed from Jesus, but the awesome thing is that we can make a new commitment right now. God is so ready and willing to step back in and become the Lord of our lives as soon as we ask Him.

If you feel as though you need to recommit your life to God, I want to encourage you to get out some paper or a journal and write down your thoughts on what you feel was making you stray away from God. Then, offer up a prayer to God and tell Him honestly how you feel. Tell God you're sorry for straying away from His truth and ask Him to become Lord over your life once again. Also, ask Him for the daily strength to surrender to His will and to walk with Him no matter what life's circumstances are.

ONE MORE THING...

If you made either one of these commitments today, you've taken the first step to changing the world. Tell someone! It's not something to be ashamed about but something to celebrate. Thank you, for listening to God's voice in your life. Because you've done that you're going to spend eternity with him forever.

My Own Thoughts

_____

_____

_____

_____

_____

_____

_____

So, you've taken the first step and you've said yes to God. What next? Well, God made it very clear what we're to do after we've said yes to Him in Romans 12:1-2. It says:

> "So here's what I want you to do, God helping you: Take your everyday, ordinary life – your sleeping, eating, going-to-work, and walking-around life – and place it before God as an offering. Embracing what God does for you is the best thing you can do for Him. Don't become so well adjusted to your culture that you fit into it without even thinking. Instead, fix your attention on God. You'll be changed from the inside out. Readily recognize what He wants from you, and quickly respond to it. Unlike the culture around you, always dragging you down to its level of immaturity, God brings the best out of you, develops well-formed maturity in you." (Msg)

I absolutely love the way this verse is translated in *The Message*. It's like God lays out exactly what He wants from us after we've accepted Him into our lives. It's not all high-tech and complicated, but it's simple and straightforward. **Place your life before God as an offering. Abandon the world around you. Embrace what God has done for you and what He's still waiting to do for you.**

— — —

A PREDETERMINED MISSION: THE CHANCE TO MAKE HISTORY

COME WITH A BROKEN SPIRIT

Jesus, I am broken now
Before You I fall, I lay me down
All I want is You, my all
– Lyrics from the song "Pray" sung by Rebecca St. James

So what does it mean to place our everyday lives before God? It means we have to cultivate a spirit of brokenness. Our society tends to tell us over and over that we need to be in total control of our lives. We're supposed to be in control of our emotions, our relationships, our behavior, and even our physical appearances. With society sending us these messages over and over, we slowly begin to build a wall around our spirit that keeps the Holy Spirit from coming in and taking Its rightful position in our lives. When we accept Christ into our lives we're saying, "I want You to become the ruler of my life." Yet, every day we quickly and quietly attempt to take matters into our hands and slowly begin to take back control over certain areas in our lives that we think we have some kind of right to.

Like I said before, God will never push us into anything, so once we've made the mistake of "regaining control," we have to voluntarily give that control up again to the Holy Spirit. We might have to do it every week for one area of our lives, and we might have to do it every hour for another area of our lives. Whatever the case, doing this is going to take a broken spirit. I know that a broken spirit sounds like something sad and depressing. But in relation to Christ, a broken spirit is one of the most beautiful and fulfilling things we can have. When I say "broken," I don't mean "crushed, trampled, and full of sorrow." God certainly does not desire those things of our spirit. But rather, when I say "broken spirit," I'm referring to a spirit that is so overwhelmed and humbled by the grace of God that it has nothing left to do but lay itself down and allow God to make Himself sovereign in that person's life from that moment on. A broken spirit lets go of every earthly and selfish desire and allows God to take them away and replace them with His perfect will.

So, after we lay down our lives before God as an offering (and as we continue to do so), we are then told to fix our attention on God, while at the same time becoming foreigners to culture's routine manner. Thought I was crazy back when I said we had to abandon the ways of our generation? God said it first.

And He meant it. He doesn't want us to settle for the quality of life that mainstream society is offering us. He created us to accomplish more than we're being offered! He hates to see us miss out on the plan that He's had for us even before we existed. What a waste it is of God's amazing preparation and creation when we go through life without ever finding out exactly what He wants of us. And when we fix our attention on God and what He's doing, it will become an easier and easier task to leave the world behind.

In his book My Utmost for His Highest, Oswald Chambers describes it like this: "Whenever the realization of God comes, even in the faintest way imaginable, be determined to recklessly abandon yourself, surrendering everything to Him. It is only through abandonment of yourself and your circumstances that you will recognize Him. You will only recognize His voice more clearly through recklessness—being willing to risk your all."

We must be willing to risk it all. We can't expect to see a change if we're cautious and wary of what we might have to sacrifice. It has to be all or nothing.

So what's the next step? The next step is identifying the areas in which we must make an effort to change. We can't try to change unless we know the things we're trying to change. Some areas that I'm going to bring up I've struggled a lot more with than others but they're all a part of my life and God is beginning to show me how I must deal with each one. In the next chapters, I'm going to be identifying specific issues that have become more than relevant in the lives of young people today. They've become issues that society has taken and twisted into lies all around. Well, no offense to society, but it's time to pinpoint the truth.

My Own Thoughts
In your opinion, what are the biggest areas that your generation needs to work on? Why do you feel so?

_____

_____

_____

_____

_____

_____

_____

ON THE PATH TO MAKING HISTORY
A summary of what I've said so far just to make sure you didn't miss a point

- We were born in our generation for a reason.
- Society has set up many standards that have caused the world to turn away from the Truth.

- It's time for our generation to change those standards by raising the bar and leading the world back to the real, authentic truth that only comes from God.

- A change so huge and revolutionary will not happen at the drop of a hat and will take time, patience, and determination, and first and foremost it will take you.

- We have a responsibility to make it happen and we simply cannot ignore that calling in our lives.

- The first step is saying "yes" to God and making Him the Lord of your lives by confessing your sin and asking Him to his home in our hearts and save us from a fallen world of sin.

- The second step is placing our everyday lives before God. This takes constant surrender to Him and must cover every area in our lives. We must hold nothing back, trying to keep some control for ourselves, but we must offer God every single area of our lives. This takes a broken spirit that has become humbled to the grace of God and has softened to His whisper. It has said, "I'm a useless vessel without You, God. Take me, use me, mold me, and change me. I am Yours."

- The third step is fixing our eyes on the Father, abandoning the ways of the world, and seeking after the ways of God. Only when we keep our eyes strictly on God will turning away from the world become easier.

- We now have to recognize the areas in life that I feel God is calling us to make some changes to. It will take sacrifices and it will take work. It doesn't matter. We were made for this.

Chapter 3

What's Love Got To Do With It?
A Lot!

1 Corinthians 13:5, "…Love…isn't always 'me first'…"

THE WORLD'S CHEAP MESSAGE OF LOVE
Like I've said before…the world's got it all wrong

At one point in our childhood we realized that there's a brand new stage of life awaiting us as soon as we get over *Babysitters Club* books and Barbies. So as soon as we feel we're too "mature" for our easy-bake ovens and stuffed animals, we dive out of our innocent kiddy pool of childhood, and immediately splash into the wavering, out-of-control ocean of young adulthood. We're sure that our lives are going to be just like Kelly's from *Saved by the Bell* and that as soon as we step into high school Zach will be waiting for us at our locker with his perfect hair and charming smile. Let the fun times begin! We're pretty sure that we *couldn't* have arrived quicker. We're ready. Bring it on, life.

CONFESSIONS OF A GIRL

I'm going to go out on a limb and say that one of the first things we want to experience in our new, "cool," "grown-up" surroundings is romantic relationships. We *have* our girlfriends to tell whether or not we look fat in a certain pair of jeans. We *have* our girlfriends to goof around with and act stupid with. But that's not enough. Now we want boyfriends. I'm going to go out on a ledge again and say that romantic relationships are also one of the biggest areas of our lives in which we've strayed from the Gold's plan. Real love has become distorted to the point where we don't even know what it means.

The other night I was driving home from church and the song *"What's Luv?"* sung by Ashanti and Fat Joe came on the radio. I (did) really like this song for some reason. I wasn't necessarily pondering over the words but it's an easy song for me (being slightly disabled in the area of singing) to sing along to. Plus, I liked the tune, the beat, etc. (Note that I'm making some pretty wonderful excuses here.)

> *Anyways, I was singing along to the chorus,*
> *(Really the only words I know to the song) which asks*
> *"What's love got to do with it?"*

Suddenly, a thought entered my mind. *You know...that's just the message that my generation is being given today. What does true love have to do with it? Think about yourself.* While the "trust" part of the song rocks, well, the selfishness that's displayed in the rest of the chorus eats away at that little speck of light in what I discovered to be a false melody of lies.

We're being sent the same message from every direction today. It comes from movies, from song lyrics, from TV shows, from magazines, and so on. The very people we look up to are even giving us the message. So many of the most popular celebrities go from relationship to relationship like it's some kind of hobby. One day they're married and the next day they aren't. One day they're dating so and so and then the next day they're seen with their new movie costar or backup dancer. Divorce rates are at an all-time high. The true meaning of love has been casually thrown into the trash and romance has been molded over into something you'd find at a cheap hotel with bright pink neon signs that flash on and off through the night. Getting involved in romantic relationships has become a selfish way of fulfilling deepdown desires and attempts to heal broken hearts and deep wounds. The world tells us it's all about ourselves. *Forget about true love. Think about yourself. Act based on how you feel, not on what's right. Live for the moment. True love takes too long. It's too much work. It takes too much commitment. You shouldn't have to go through any real labor like that. You deserve this* now.

Not only are we getting the wrong message but we're also getting plenty of mixed messages. We're being told one thing, and then the next second we're being told a totally opposite thing from the same source! I was looking at an old magazine from months earlier and I came across an ad warning against teen pregnancy that was supposedly either trying to convince me to have no sex at all, or "safe sex," which is such an oxymoron because there's no such thing as safe sex until you're married. As I was flipping through the same magazine, only a different issue from a few months later, I came across an article entitled, "The first time," with a picture of a guy and a girl wrapped in each other's arms in bed. *Whoa, whoa, whoa. I thought just a few pages earlier they were telling me not to have sex?* The article was one big survey with questions like "What was the first time like for you?" and "Where was YOUR first time?" and "What advice would you give about the first time?" It was like the magazine was giving two totally different messages: a) Be smart and don't have sex until you're married or you might end up pregnant, and b) People your age are having sex. Here's some advice. The messages were mixed and totally contradictory. And even though the magazine never came right out and said "It's OK to have sex" or "Don't have sex at all," both the ad and the article had a way of speaking for themselves and to me, the messages were clear, yet completely opposite of each other.

I wish so badly that every young person could realize that the message of love from the world is so false. There's something authentic, there's something more, something real.

I really think it's sad the way that so many young people are carelessly throwing themselves into relationship after relationship searching for acceptance, love, and someone to tell them they're beautiful and cherished. We dream of that special someone to pick us up in their arms and call us a princess. There's a longing deep down in our hurting hearts for a knowledge that we matter to *someone*, to know that *someone* out there smiles when they think of us, that someone out there is dreaming of us, and that *someone* out there is missing us every time we're not with them.

Unfortunately, to fill the void in our hearts we take the first person that comes along and attempt to be fulfilled by someone that really can't fill the void we're looking to fill. And if no one *does* come along, we begin to daydream about it, which turns into an obsession, and finally turns into a hurt because we feel unwanted and rejected by the opposite sex. It's a trap.

– – –

WHAT'S LOVE GOT TO DO WITH IT? A LOT!

A Little bit of my own Story
Sometimes a personal testimony is the best way to paint a picture

Honestly, relationships were a huge part of my (so far) high school experience. (At the time I'm writing this I still have one year left.) And the weird thing is, I've only really "gone out" with two different guys. (By the way, someone really needs to change the term "going out"…that, or get its definition in a dictionary so that there's no more nationwide confusion.) The first guy was in ninth grade, and the second guy was in tenth grade. I'm not going to go into long, boring details about the relationships but I do want to say that at both times I thought I was definitely mature enough for a relationship. I thought I had my life on track with God and that it was totally fine that I was giving so much time into each relationship. I was still a good Christian. No harm done. Or so I thought.

Well, the relationships ended in different ways. One time I was the heart breaker and the other time I was the one with the broken heart. Needless to say, it doesn't matter who does the breaking up. High school breakups, well, to put it plain, they stink big time. It's a little different in 6th grade when you "go out" (there's that phrase again) with a guy for a few weeks, talk to him on the phone a few times, and if the relationship is *really* "serious" you might even hold hands a few times. Even though it's very true that you can become emotionally attached to someone at such a young age, it's a lot less likely. Whereas in high school, relationships get a lot more serious and we tend to attach ourselves to the person we're dating and instantly they become a part of who we are.

I want you to know that I'm not speaking for everybody, because not all high school relationships go this way. But the fact is, the majority of teenage relationships do, and that's why I want to bring it up.

Anyways, relationships in high school are a huge thing and I firmly believe that one of God's biggest desires is for this generation and the generations to come to change the way we go about them. What God has to say about love is so much different from what the world has been telling us for who knows how long. In the past two years, God has spoken to me a tremendous amount about relationships and through quite a long process He's brought me closer and closer to His will for that area in my life. Honestly, I still struggle a huge amount in this area of my life, but I want to share with you what God has told me so far and what I believe He's calling us towards.

In the fall of my sophomore year in high school, my church attended a weekend-long youth convention. I was really looking forward to it. Hundreds of area youth groups and individuals gathered together for awesome worship, dramas, and an awesome speaker. It had been about a month since my last boyfriend and I had broken up, and I still wasn't sure exactly where I stood on relationships. To me, it was still an area in my life where the water was muddy and unclear. I was oblivious to just how much I still needed to learn. But, seriously, how much does God have to say about relationships? I mean, as long as I end up with a Christian guy who loves the Lord in the end, why does it matter if I have a few innocent relationships along the way? I had already established that I was saving sex for marriage, and there was simply no question about it: I would *never* let my guard down when it came to having sex before marriage. But I was soon to learn that in God's eyes, there's so much more to relationships than just sex. Of course, God still sees it as a huge deal, but in today's culture, often even in the church, abstinence has become the

WHAT'S LOVE GOT TO DO WITH IT? A LOT!

main focus on relationships. *Whatever you do and no matter who you're with, just* don't *have sex before marriage.*

Anyways, we got to the convention and what do you think the topic of the weekend was? Yep, you guessed it. Relationships. It really did intrigue me. We were given challenges such as "crush the crush" and the second session we were given a bigger challenge that I'd say changed my life forever. We were given the challenge to "date God for a year." It sounds really weird doesn't it? Let me explain. The challenge was for us to not date anyone for the next year, and totally commit ourselves to God. No more flirting, or "innocent" three-hour phone calls with our crushes. It was a year to hang out with God and get to know Him in ways we never had before. At the end of the message, the speaker was praying for us and then, after he had made the challenge clear, he told us, "If God has spoken to you and you are ready to take on this challenge, I'd like you to stand up in your seat. I'd like to say a special prayer over you." Oh, shoot. I knew he was going to say that.

The truth was, God had gotten a hold of my heart that weekend, and He had made it plain and clear to me that I needed to make some major changes in my love life. After hearing the challenge, I began to hear that still, small voice in my heart and it was clearly saying, *"This is for you, this is for you." OK God, I guess you know what you're doing. Besides, I think I could really use a year off. Hey, this will be good. I can do this.* Enthusiastic about what God had revealed to me in the previous message, I slowly stood to my feet. In my opinion, the message was strong and convincing, which is why I was expecting so many more people to stand up. Well, my eyes must have been closed when I stood up, because all I can remember is opening my eyes and being totally stunned. There was hardly *anyone* standing. It was nowhere near even half of the people in the stadium. *Tessa! What are you doing?* I thought to myself. Suddenly, I felt totally stupid. There I was, the only girl in my youth group standing and feeling like a banana in the midst of thirty oranges. After the prayer I sat down and thought to myself: *Just what exactly are you getting yourself into?*

The convention ended on a Saturday night and the next day at church one of my youth sponsors who had not been able to attend told me that she heard about the commitment I had made and thought it was really awesome. The encouragement, well, encouraged me, to say the least, and I remained eager to begin the year ahead of me. It started off great, but it soon became a huge struggle for me. The convention was in November and by December I was really feeling the heat. Somewhere between December 17 and December 21 (I forgot to write the date that day) I wrote in my journal:

This is what I'm struggling with. I'm focusing almost 24/7 on guys when I'm supposed to be taking a year off and dating God.

Then again on January 4:

This year is going well but tonight I went ice skating with some friends and seeing all the couples really made me want a boyfriend.

I was trying, but I wasn't trying hard enough. By February, I had a stupid crush on the guy I asked to homecoming (our school did it Sadie Hawkins style that year where the girls ask the guys). I hardly even knew him but my friends convinced me to ask him and that was that. I guess you could say that I wasn't sticking very well to my commitment. I knew inside that I wasn't following it with my whole heart and that was really hard for me. Seriously, when you're a sophomore in high school it's not the coolest thing to say, "I'm dating God for a year." Without going into an hour-long explanation, it just came out weird. And unfortunately, I know there were some times when I was even embarrassed about it.

Before you know it, I meet this awesome guy. (Don't worry; he knows I'm going to tell you the story). I had actually met him a couple of years ago through my best friend and had occasionally talked to him over the Internet. Anyways, the spring after I had made my commitment we began to talk a lot. I was going through a really hard time with something else in my life at that time dealing with my health and he had been a huge encouragement to me. He was on fire for God and not to mention he was pretty cute. OK, you can probably predict the story from here. I totally fall for the guy and by June I'm head over heels in a serious crush, hence on June 22 I wrote:

Lord, while I'm supposed to be dating you,
I find myself stuck with a huge crush.

I'm going to make a long story short because giving you every detail of the year would definitely bore you. Anyways, before the year was up, I read three books that totally changed my view on relationships. God spoke to me about so many things and by the time November rolled around when I was "allowed" to date again, I really didn't even want to date. I knew it wasn't what God wanted for my life at the time and now that I knew *why* it was so much easier to go through with. Note that I didn't say it was completely effortless, because it wasn't. It still isn't. I still struggle a great deal with it. But now that God has shown me *His* view on relationships, I know in my heart what I need to be seeking after and I've come to know exactly what I need to do to follow God's plan for relationships in my life, which I came to learn is a perfectly awesome plan.

– – –

CONFESSIONS OF A GIRL

FILLING THE VOID
Do you feel the space in your heart?

Psalms 63:3, 5, "…your love is better than life…my soul will be satisfied as with the richest of foods…" (NIV)

You may not have noticed it when you were ten years old, but it probably became a little more evident in the years after. I'm talking about that empty space in your heart that suddenly desires to be filled. It's the same space in our heart that's searching for a deeper fulfillment, pleasure, and satisfaction. It was delicately placed in our hearts when God carefully and meticulously created every part of our being. He put it there for a reason, that we might come to know Him and one day let Him fill it with *His* love only. Of course He created a place in our hearts to be filled with love from our parents, friends, future spouse, etc., but *before* those spaces can be filled, we *must* fill the void that God created specifically for Himself.

To put it plainly, God wants to become our *first love and His love must fill our hearts first.* When these two things happen, a tremendous amount of fulfillment comes into our lives like nothing we've ever experienced before. It's because the void is filled. Unfortunately, too many of us have identified the void after feeling empty and unfulfilled and then tried to fill it with love and acceptance from the wrong person. In the end, we realize that that person can't fill the void any better than the last person, and we go back to feeling our vacant selves before the next person comes along and attempts to do the job.

If only we knew. If only we knew that God dropped a tear every time we pushed His love away and unsuccessfully turned to a mere human being to take His place. If only we knew that we were only making life harder for ourselves. If only we knew what we were missing out on. If only we knew.

What exactly do you mean when you say a mere *human being?* I mean that people aren't perfect and as long as we're here on earth no one ever will be. There's a sheer perfection and saving grace that God possesses that humans will never live up to while still living in a world of sin, and as harsh as that sounds, it's actually not meant to put us "mere humans" down at all. It's only said to put us in our rightful place. If people were perfect and able to fulfill our every need, where would that leave room in our lives for the saving grace of God? Our peers, our parents, and our friends will someday let us down. It's simply expected of them because they're only humans. And there's still a huge amount of room in our lives for love from and towards these people, but we *have* to come to grips with the fact that God is the perfect form of love, only His love can completely fulfill our lives, and until He is the very first and foremost love in our lives, we'll never really be loving the way we were made to love.

When we let someone else fill that void in our hearts it's like we're telling God that for some reason He's not enough. God not being enough? It's the biggest lie that Satan could ever tell us. To let God fill that void in our hearts that only He can fill is like a complete turn away from the world and that's why Satan hates it so much. He does everything in his power to keep us from falling into the arms of Jesus and giving in to His love.

Before a couple of years ago, I had never heard the phrase "falling in love with Jesus." *Fall in love with Jesus? I thought I was only supposed to fall in love when I'm in a romantic relationship. I love Jesus, I love Him a lot, but how do I continue to* fall *in love with Him?* Now I know exactly what falling in love with Christ calls for and that it's an imperative part of my life. It's like when we're children, still innocent and unaware of so many things. The excuse "I didn't know any better" actually still works! But once we grow and mature to know better, we can no longer say those innocent words.

Take for example when I was about three years old. We had a ton of cats and one of them had just had babies. Being the blameless little girl that I was, I thought that I'd take one of the kittens and stuff it down one of my dad's big work boots. (I don't know what ever happened to that cat but wherever you are, I'm sorry!) I didn't realize that you just couldn't stuff little kittens down into boots where they could hardly breathe. My parents didn't yell at me and scold me because they knew I didn't know any better. Instead, they gently let me off the hook and probably told me, "Now Tessa, you shouldn't stuff little kitties down into daddy's boots. It's not very nice." We actually took a picture of it and it's really very funny, not that the kitten would agree. But today I know a lot better than to do something like that. Seriously, if I came to your house and stuffed your kitten down a boot, you'd think I was cruel and immature wouldn't you? I would. It kind of goes the same way in our walk with God. When we first come to know Him, we're still learning to walk in His ways and we're beginning to distinguish what sin really is. Once we begin to grow and learn what God expects of us, we don't have an excuse to go back and commit the same sins. Now I'm not saying we can never mess up, because as I said before, humans will never be perfect and we're going to mess up from time to time. But God makes it clear that once we know what's expected of us, we can't keep on doing wrong. Hebrews 10:26 says, "If we deliberately keep on sinning after we have received the knowledge of the truth, no sacrifice for sins is left." (NIV)

WHAT'S LOVE GOT TO DO WITH IT? A LOT!

Now that I know that falling in love with Jesus before anything and anyone else has to be my top priority, I can't just pretend I didn't hear it and keep on trying to claim my innocence. It won't work now and it never will.

So how exactly do you go about falling in love with such a big and powerful God? I think to do it we have to realize just *who* God is. In so many of our minds God is this big, authoritative being that's only waiting for us to sin so He can say, "There you go again, messing up!" It makes me cringe to think that that is how so many young people see God. If only we could come to know that God is not only a God of power and sovereignty, but He's also a God with the most tender and gentle of Hearts. He's the lion, *and* He's the lamb. The most intimate and romantic relationship out there is a love relationship with Jesus Christ. It goes wider than the ocean and it contains more love than the deepest of seas. God cherishes us like we could never imagine! He *never* fails us. His love is perfect, and eternally *unconditional*. How could you *not* fall in love with Him? How could you *not*, after a hard and stressful day, just fall into His arms and let His loving peace fall over you like rain? One thing I know for sure, there is *no* love like the love of Jesus. I don't care if you think you have the sweetest and most romantic guy out there, it doesn't even compare to the attributes of God's love.

To realize who God is we have to spend time with Him. We have to talk to Him and really get to know Him and we also have to cultivate a heart that's willing to listen to Him speak to us. We have to *desire from deep within* to fall in love with Jesus or else it's never going to happen. In a world that is calling for our attention from a zillion different directions, spending time to get to know someone so much takes a lot of discipline. Our generation has definitely become expert at one thing: staying busy. Once we get to high school we're opened up to an entire new world of things that can easily take up our time. There's clubs, sports, which become extremely time consuming in high school, after school jobs, homework, and on top of all that we have a family and a social life to keep up on. Some of the schedules of my friends are absolutely nuts! I know kids that leave for school at seven in the morning and sometimes don't get home until eight or nine at night, with homework that's yet to be finished. By eleven or twelve after they've done their homework and either chatted on the Internet with friends or watched a favorite TV show (or both at once), they're ready to crash.

If you wait until the very end of the day to spend time with God, when all you're thinking about is getting some shut-eye before repeating your daily routine all over again, I can assure you, it's not going to be very effective. So many times I've planned on spending time with God before I went to bed, only to wait until after I'd heard the "necessary" gossip on the Internet. I then attempt to climb into bed and read my Bible, write in my journal, or pray before my attention span shuts down for the night. But by that time, it's too late. I'm already a goner. As my eyes are drifting down the pages, they slowly shut and my brain goes off into wonderland. I'll half-heartedly open my eyes and try to read again, but before you know it I'm half asleep once again. By that time, I'll give up. I'll then whisper an ashamed "sorry" up to Heaven and fall to sleep. Only to do it again the next day.

Well, I've come to realize that it can't work that way. If I don't take my love relationship with Jesus seriously, I'll never get to the point where I've fallen completely in love with Him and I'll never come to the point where His love is ultimately the only thing I need. We have to spend time with God at a time when we're *ready* and *expectant* to hear from Him. Our hearts have to be open to His word and our minds can't be wandering off thinking about what we're going to wear the next day or what we're going to eat for lunch. Now, I know people my age don't have huge attention spans. I'm pretty sure they're as big as a three-year-old's. With that in mind, we have to choose a time in the day when we won't be easily distracted by anything around us. It should be a consistent time of day that we know we'll always have open and one where we know we won't be interrupted. If you choose a time when your friends usually like to call, you might even want to let them know that every day you're going to be busy for that certain period of time. We have to learn to completely shut out the world around us and solely focus on God. The time of day is going to be different for everyone.

This past year I was able to develop the habit of getting up before school and for twenty to thirty minutes spending time with God. I have to admit, there were mornings when all I felt like doing was pressing the snooze button and going back to sleep, and there were some mornings I did just that. There were also some mornings when I sat on the couch and barely focused at all on what I was saying or reading either because I hadn't made myself go to bed early enough to get up that morning, or because I was simply being lazy and not putting all of my effort and attention into what I was doing. Some people might be better off spending time with God after school, which may mean not joining a certain after-school club. Others may be most focused at around eight in the evening, which may mean giving up watching a certain TV show. I don't know what the case is for you, but I do know that if we're totally serious about falling in love with Christ, there are going to be sacrifices that we must be willing to make along the way.

Once spending time with God becomes part of our daily routine, we'll begin to want more and more of Him, and less and less of the world. To come to that place, where all we want is God, is one of the most wonderful feelings in the world. Coming to know the nature of God takes an entire lifetime. There will always be more to discover, more secrets that He'll reveal to us about Himself. Falling in love with Christ and who He is, is a thrilling and exhilarating experience that will capture our hearts and redirect our energies and concerns.

I encourage you to seek with all your heart to fall in love with Christ. Spend time with Him daily. Study His word. Take notes, write your thoughts down. Keep a journal of how God is working in your life. Study different versions of the Bible to get different interpretations of a verse. And lastly, *communicate* with God. Pour out your heart to God! Even though He already knows how we feel and what we're going through, He still desires for us to tell Him.

One of my favorite stories in the Bible is about a woman who was going through a very hard time in her life. Her name was Hannah and her story is found in 1 Samuel 1. Hannah longed to give birth to a child but she was unable to become pregnant. At one point Hannah fell on her knees and wept loudly to God and cried out to Him in prayer, pleading for God to allow her to bear a child. Hannah's lips were moving in great fervor but no words were coming out of her mouth, instead they were flowing hastily out of her heart with a passion that only comes from knowing God. The priest nearby, whose name was Eli, mistook Hannah for being drunk and asked her just how long she would keep it up. Hannah replied, "I am a woman who is deeply troubled…I was pouring out my soul to the Lord." (1 Samuel 1:15, NIV) Hannah had an intimate relationship with Christ and was not ashamed to come before the throne of God and weep at his feet. God longs for us to come before Him as Hannah did and pour out our souls. And pouring out our souls to God should not only take place during a time of sorrow and grief, but also during times of joy and gratitude. God wants us to pour out our dreams, our fears, our concerns, our smallest joys, and our deepest gratitude to Him. This kind of communication with God, unleashed, pure, honest communication, will bring us all the more closer to Him.

Do you know what I'm talking about now? Do you know the void in your heart that you've been trying to fill with other loves or more specifically, a romantic relationship with someone? I'm going to guess that if you have tried to fill that void with another love, your heart was never completely filled, and you were still left longing for more. The only reason I can tell you that is because God has revealed to me that unless *God* and *God alone* is filling the void in our hearts that He placed there for Himself, we will always be hungering for more.

I want to encourage you right now. Take some time to talk to God. If you haven't yet let Him fill the void in your heart, whether you've been searching in other places or not, ask Him to fill that void. I can promise you, if you're totally and completely serious about it, God *will* listen and He *will* fill that void. We only have to come with open hearts and willingness to do whatever He asks of us. After you ask God to fill that void in your heart, ask Him to reveal to you every other thing that you have used to try and fill the void. It might be a romantic relationship that left you broken and hurt. It might be a romantic relationship that you know has drawn you further from the Lord. It might be a romantic relationship that has taken up so much of your time that you've stopped spending time with God. It might not even be a romantic relationship at all. Whatever it is, confess it to God and ask for forgiveness for trying to fill your heart with something that took over God's rightful place.

Also, ask God to reveal to you some sacrifices you may need to begin to make that will enable you to spend more time with Him and seek Him wholeheartedly. Write down what God reveals to you and ask Him to give you the strength and humility that you'll need to listen to Him and obey what He's asking of you. I promise you, no matter how huge the sacrifice may seem, it will be so worth it in the end. It may cause some tears, it may cost some of your popularity, and it may cost going against what every other person expects of you. I'm almost sure it will cost *something*. Why? Because the world doesn't flow in the same direction as God. What He asks of us is going to be the opposite of what the world is telling us to do. Yes, that makes it all the more hard, but it also makes the journey with Christ all the more exciting and adventurous. God has *so* much more to offer than the world! When we realize this truth to its full, we are on our way to a relationship of freedom, deep love, and fulfillment.

— — —

My Own Thoughts

_____

_____

_____

_____

_____

_____

WE MISSED A SPOT!
Something even your best sex ed teacher may not have told you

It seems that over the past few years there has been a lot of awareness raising about teen pregnancy, abstinence, etc. When I was in 8th grade a woman came in and did a presentation encouraging abstinence. She gave one student a cup of chocolate pudding and another student a cup of vanilla pudding. She told them to put all the pudding in one cup and mix it all together. She then said, "OK, now separate the vanilla pudding from the chocolate pudding. It (very obviously) wasn't going to work. Her point was that once you have sex with someone, you're a part of that person forever. You've given away a part of your body that you'll never get back. The point of the presentation was good. We heard statistics about STDs, teen pregnancy rates, and so on. We even got these sweet pens that said, "Put out the fire on your sexual desire." I remember when the same group went to my older sister's class. They gave her the saying, "Control your urgin', be a virgin." Corny, I know, and I'm sure there were plenty of jokes that day.

The following year in my 9th grade speech class a girl did a persuasive speech on abstinence. She started off her speech by telling us to imagine that it was Christmas morning. We had jumped out of bed full of excitement and we were as eager as little kids to see what Santa Claus had brought us. However, when we entered the living room, we saw a disastrous sight. Our presents had already been opened. The wrapping paper was thrown all over the room and the ribbon had lost its curl. And worse! The presents were used! She then made the connection between the opened present and a person who, before their wedding night, has already lost their virginity. The precious gift had already been opened and used. The mystery was gone, the excitement ruined. I thought it was an awesome example. In the rest of her speech she explained why saving sex for marriage was the best choice. She not only warned of STDs and pregnancy but she also made us aware that there are a lot of emotional consequences as well, such as depression. It really was a great speech.

Finally, in my 10th grade Health class a group came to my school and gave a pretty humorous and yet convincing message on why we should *save sex for marriage*! What I liked about it was that the group was made up of people my age. They were going through the same thing I was. Their presentation was creative, entertaining, and held my attention until the end.

So, why did I just tell you about every sex ed speech I've heard since I was fourteen? No, I wasn't just trying to fill up pages with something that related to the topic. The point that was made in each presentation formed a continuous pattern. The point made in *every* one of those sex ed speeches was that I should *save sex for marriage*. (Duh, you're saying.) But that's just it! That's the *only* message we're getting in regard to relationships today! And honestly, before I learned what I did, I thought that's all there was to it. I thought "pure" was another word for "virgin." Let me tell you, there's *so* much more to purity than just not having sex!

As extremely important and relevant as the message of abstinence is, it's only a part of the message that young people need to hear about relationships. I think as a whole, Christians have left out a huge point when educating young people on what God desires of them. **We not only have to guard our bodies, but we have to guard our *hearts*.** Our heart is the deepest part of our being. It's where our every secret lies. It's the very core of who we are. Without a heart, we'd be emotionless people walking around without a purpose. Our heart is the homeland of our dreams, our fears, and every other imaginable emotion. Unfortunately, this part of the whole "save yourself for your future spouse" idea has been left out of the message. However, I think it's so extremely important that we realize what it means to guard our hearts and why it's such an important part of relationships.

— — —

WHAT'S LOVE GOT TO DO WITH IT? A LOT!

UNDER MY SLEEVE, PLEASE
Where do you wear your heart?

Proverbs 4:23, "Above all else, guard your heart, for it is the wellspring of life." (NIV)
Proverbs 4:23, "Keep vigilant watch over your heart..."
(Msg)

Only in the past year have I learned what it means to guard my heart, and I'll try to explain the best I can. I do know that God commands it in Proverbs 4:23 and I also know that if God commands it, it's *very* worthwhile to listen to it. The verse has taken a whole new significance to me and now it really means a lot to me. So what does it mean to guard your heart? I think I'll start off by saying a little about what it *doesn't* mean.

Have you ever heard someone accuse another person of "wearing their heart on their sleeve?" Maybe they weren't even saying it as a negative thing, but just as a comment. I guess people don't really say it that much. But I do know the phrase exists! You can trust me on that one even if you've never heard it. Anyways, I thought about what the phrase was getting at. What does it mean? I even asked my mom what she thought the phrase meant. She pondered over it for a few seconds and hesitantly decided that she really didn't know what people meant when they said that. Of course, she had some ideas about what they meant, but she wasn't sure.

When you hear the phrase you might think of a girl that's loud, flirtatious, says exactly what she thinks, and jumps from relationship to relationship. That's the first idea I got when I heard it. And if someone were to ask me a year ago if I was the kind of girl that wore my heart on my sleeve I would have said definitely not. I'm a very quiet person. I'm never the life of the party. I never have very witty things to say and I can never come up with good comeback lines. I'm often insecure and I'm not outgoing enough to flirt. If flirting is a talent, well, I'm definitely lacking in that department. Little did I know, though, that I even though I wasn't fitting my definition of that kind of girl, I still wasn't guarding my heart very well. I had a lot to learn.

If you were to ask me what the phrase meant today, I'd tell you that I think wearing your heart on your sleeve is the exact opposite of guarding it. If it's out there on your "sleeve," it's there for everyone to see. Anyone can take it. It's exposed. If you're guarding it carefully, no one can take it from you, and no one can look into it without your permission.

When we're not keeping close watch over our heart in a relationship, we end up giving something away that should be kept for our future spouse. How can you give your heart away, anyways? It's really not all that hard, but the cost is great. Our hearts are so full of emotion, and as girls, it's so easy for us to take all of those emotions and get all of them wrapped up into a relationship to the point where we become emotionally attached to the guy we're dating.

I'm not saying that a relationship can't be emotional, because any relationship is going to bring out plenty of emotions. What I am saying is that it's wrong to put so much emotion into a relationship with someone that you're not going to spend the rest of your life with. When the breakup comes after you've become so emotionally attached to someone, it literally rips your heart out and that person takes a piece of it with them that you can never get back. A piece that was meant only for your future spouse.

I'm an extremely emotional person so this concept is hard for me. I'm also a pretty deep person, which leads to my next thought. The thoughts that go off inside of my head can be extremely complicated; even I don't understand them sometimes. But I do like to talk about deep things with other people. Before, I thought it was no problem that I was spilling out so many thoughts from my heart to guys. There have been a few guys in my life that I've told so many things to: my deepest dreams, parts of my past, secrets about who I *really* am. There are a few guys out there that probably know me better than even my best girlfriends. I haven't been in a romantic relationship with all of them, but even so, all of those guys have a part of me that I wish I had saved entirely for my future husband.

Besides our relationship with Christ, marriage is the most intimate relationship on earth and God purposely created marriage so that we could share our complete being with someone. Part of saving ourselves for our future spouse is saving the deepest parts of our hearts, including the part of our heart that is for our Lord only. When we save our hearts for our future spouses, the intimacy of our coming marriage to that person will be all the more beautiful. A guy that's exposed every part of his emotional self to dozens of other girls is not going to be the first guy I look at when I'm looking for a future husband. Likewise, we need to be sure that in our relationships before marriage we're holding steadfast to Christ, and always making sure that He is the first and foremost fulfillment of all of our emotional needs. We can also spill *anything* and *everything* out to God. Just like Hannah in 1 Samuel as I mentioned before, we can pour out our hearts to God! When we pour out our hearts to a guy that we're romantically involved with, only for the relationship to end in a breakup, whether it be a harsh breakup or not, we'll feel as though that guy took something from us that we can't get back. Suddenly we'll feel as if we've exposed ourselves to someone that's no longer a part of our lives in the same way.

I don't think it only goes for romantic relationships. We need to keep a firm grasp on what we share with the opposite sex in general. This might sound like a totally absurd suggestion, and that's why I want to make sure you really understand what I'm saying. First of all, I'm not proposing that you don't have any friends of the opposite sex. That would be a ridiculous thing to ask of you. Being able to have both guy and girl friends, especially at this age, is one of the best things about growing up and realizing that guys actually don't have cooties. Second, I'm not proposing that you develop a bunch of surface relationships that are only, well, on the surface. I'm not suggesting that you just pretend to be somebody else and hide your real self from your friends. That's the worst thing that you could do. Being real and honest is a huge part of any relationship. Thirdly, I'm not suggesting that all of our relationships with the opposite sex, romantic or not, should never involve any emotions. That would be impossible!

What I *am* saying is that when we enter into a relationship with the opposite sex, we have to keep the future in mind. Ask yourself, "Am I giving away a part of my heart that's only meant to be given to my future spouse?"

We not only have to keep our future in mind in regard to our hearts, but we also have to keep in mind the part of our hearts that I mentioned earlier, the part that only God can fill. As soon as a relationship with the opposite sex is taking reign over our love relationship with Jesus, we know that we're not guarding our hearts the way God desires us to. Remember that God must become our first and foremost love. When *anything* or *anyone* gets in the way of that, we can be sure right there and then that somewhere we're compromising.

The good news is that we can have awesome relationships with the opposite sex without compromising. We just have to make sure that God is at the center of those relationships and that we're giving Him glory in everything we do and say.

WHAT'S LOVE GOT TO DO WITH IT? A LOT!

THAT EVER-POPULAR QUESTION
We ask it over and over...what's the answer?

1 Corinthians 6:19, "Do you not know that your body is a temple of the Holy Spirit, who is in you, whom you have received from God? You are not your own."

Now that I've addressed the issue of guarding your heart, I want to go back to the physical realm of relationships. I think it's definitely the part we've heard the most about when it comes to relationships, especially when you've reached the point where holding hands isn't something so big that everybody's talking about it at recess and that kissing someone isn't something that only happens after you've been doubled dared. I've already talked about not having sex and I'm really not going to elaborate on that now because we've heard it over and over and over. *Save sex for marriage. Abstinence, abstinence, abstinence.* I don't want you to get the idea that I don't think it's important to save sex for marriage, because I think it's extremely important, one of the most important parts of any romantic relationship. I've committed to abstinence before marriage and I plan on sticking with that promise. But what about everything physical *besides* sex? What about little things like a goodnight kiss and what about things that push right to the border of officially losing your virginity? It brings me to the ever-popular question that everyone wants to know the answer to: How far is too far?

In my youth group, we've talked about the relationship issue a number of times, and this question has caused a lot of debate. I've heard comments like "don't do anything below the neck" and "if you couldn't do it in front of your parents, it's too far." You have to admit, the answer seems to be very gray, in the midst of black and white answers to so many other issues. So if we can't settle the debate with an absolute answer, God *must* have an exact answer somewhere in the Bible. Well, that's right and it's wrong. God never *directly* answers the question in the Bible. None of the Ten Commandments say, "Thou shall do nothing but kiss before marriage." When we're first looking for an exact answer in the Bible, only to come up with nothing, our first thought might be, "If God didn't come right out and address the issue I guess that means He doesn't really care too much about it." Wrong. God cares a tremendous amount.

God didn't give us a specific set of physical boundaries. Instead, He gave us two single commandments that we can ultimately use to base our physical relationships on. In Matthew 22:37-39: "Jesus replied: 'Love the Lord your God with all your heart and with all your soul and with all your mind. This is the first and greatest commandment. And the second is like it: Love your neighbor as yourself'." When we get involved in a physical relationship we *must* keep these commandments in mind.

God's command to love each other can again be found in John 13:34 when Jesus says, "A new command I give you: Love one another. As I have loved you, so you must love one another." (NIV) Again, in John 15:17 Jesus says, "This is my command: Love each other." (NIV) God is so serious about us *loving* each other. Look how many times He mentioned it in the Bible. He even called it His *second* greatest commandment to humankind. When we become physically involved with someone in a romantic relationship we have the choice to listen to that commandment or completely ignore it.

How far you choose to take the physical part of your relationship is going to be your own choice. Some girls have chosen to not kiss a guy until their wedding date, and some girls feel that kissing isn't that big a deal. I'm not going to give you a list of my own specific convictions because everyone is going to be convinced differently in all kinds of situations. You might want to make a list of your own personal convictions and your own boundaries. But apart from making specific rules, always be sure to ask yourself these questions:

- Is what I'm doing loving to the other person regarding their future?
- Is what I'm doing loving to this person's future spouse?
- Is what I'm doing honoring my own body and the body of the other person?
- Is what I'm doing loving to my future spouse?
- Is what I'm doing honorable in God's sight?

— — —

Look at Your Life

I've talked about two different areas in relationships: the emotional part where the heart gets involved and the physical part where the body is involved. To reflect on each of these things I want to encourage you to right now take a look at your relationships with the opposite sex. Ask yourself these questions and be completely honest in your answers. You may want to take some time to write the answers in a journal so that you can reflect further on each question. Also, talk to God about your relationships with the opposite sex and ask Him to help you see things through His eyes.

- What would God have to say about my relationships with the opposite sex?
- What would my future husband have to say?
- Would he be jealous? Why?

- Would God be jealous? Why?
- Am I giving myself away physically, and just as important, am I giving myself away emotionally? How?
- Is there a relationship that I need to change in my life in order to totally guard my heart as God commands in Proverbs 4:23?
- Am I aware of my own physical boundaries?
- Do I make sure that the guys I date are aware of my own physical boundaries?
- Are the guys I date on the same page as me when it comes to God's plan for how we handle relationships?

When you make the decision to totally honor God in every area of your relationships with the opposite sex, both physically and emotionally, God will honor that decision and give you the strength you need to carry out your decision. If you do make the decision to honor God in every aspect of your relationships with the opposite sex, I can assure you this right now: most of the world around you is not going to be cheering you on. Because like I said before, the world doesn't flow in the same direction as God. God's calling us for something bigger and better, something more fulfilling than the norm. Remember…God has called you, and this entire generation, to raise the bar. Turning the wheel on how we handle relationships is a huge way in which this generation can begin to make an effect on the rest of the world. Be that first person to decide that you really don't care *what* the magazines are telling you is right, or *what* the most popular TV show is showing you is ordinary. The world will begin to take notice…things will begin to change.

- - -

WHAT'S LOVE GOT TO DO WITH IT? A LOT!

My Own Thoughts

_____

_____

_____

_____

_____

_____

TO DATE OR NOT TO DATE: THAT IS THE QUESTION
And a very hard question it may seem

OK, what does it actually mean to be dating someone, anyways? Does it mean you can call that person your boyfriend or girlfriend? Does it mean you actually go on dates? And when you're dating someone, can you go out on dates with other people? How much commitment is there when you're dating someone? Oh, how I wish I could answer those questions, but I'm not going to try because I know everyone probably has a different definition of what "dating" is in their minds. That's fine. I'm not going to try to give a set definition of the word. We don't want a bunch of controversy raised up over a stupid word.

So, I think I want to rephrase that question: "To be involved in a romantic relationship with someone of the opposite sex who's *more* than a friend or not to be involved in a romantic relationship with someone of the opposite sex who's more *than* a friend: *THAT* is the question." I thought it was a lot easier to just use the word "date," but I think you get the gist.

I really struggle with answering this question for myself. I've heard so many different opinions and ideas from different sources that it's hard to really decide on the best plan. First off, what is society telling us? I'll tell you what I'm hearing from society. I'm hearing that as soon as I realize that, gee, I'm interested in the opposite sex, I should *probably* go out and find myself a boyfriend. Now, it can't be just *any* guy. He should probably look good, and a six pack wouldn't hurt either. He should wear the right clothes and be friends with the right people. Whatever you do, don't date a loser. That's what I'm hearing. Maybe you're hearing something different, I don't know. But I do know that dating is a huge issue.

Magazines have oh-so-appealing headlines like, "Turn your crush into your boyfriend…tomorrow!" "How to catch his attention," "Are you and your crush meant to be together?" and "The ten biggest ways to get him to notice you." And then there's the *very* occasional article entitled, "It's OK to be single." I don't know about you but it's pretty hard for me to believe that it's OK for me to be single in the midst of all the other messages I'm getting.

And then there are all the different messages I'm getting about how to go about the whole dating thing. I've read and heard a lot of different things from different people. Some books tell me that courting is the best way to have a relationship with a guy. Some books tell me that it's better to just hold out from dating until I meet the guy that I believe God wants me to be with forever. Someone that I respect very much once told me that at this age, it's better to just go out on dates with a bunch of different people so that I can get an idea of the kind of guy I want to marry one day. *Who do I listen to? What's the best strategy? What does God want?* The questions are going off inside my head and creating a whirl of confusion until I realize one thing: **Before I leap into any**

dating relationship, God wants to be enough for me. God wants to be enough? Yes.

I think it is so crucial that before we get involved in any romantic relationship we answer the question, "Is God *enough* for me *right now*?" Before we can answer with an honest "yes," I really don't think we're ready for a romantic relationship. I've battled with this concept over and over. I've prayed countless times, "Lord, *please* become enough for me!" But too many times my human nature gives in to the ways of the world around me and I selfishly lose the battle. I quickly forget the magnitude of God's love for me and before I know it I'm searching for love and affirmation from a guy. As soon as I realize it I slap my hand and think, *Tessa! Don't you get it? God's love will satisfy! If no guy on earth ever tells you you're beautiful, if no guy ever tells you he thinks you're amazing, and if no guy ever picks you up in his arms with a heart-warming embrace, God's love is* still *enough*! It hits me hard every time.

I love the words to the song "Enough" by Chris Tomlin. The chorus goes like this:

> *All of You is more than enough for all of me*
> *For every thirst and every need*
> *You satisfy me with Your love*
> *And all I have in You is more than enough*

When I first heard this song, I fell in love with it. The words hold so much truth in them, a truth that I've been longing to grasp for quite some time. It's so hard to fight with the battle inside of us, telling us that we need to have a boyfriend in order to be fulfilled. But before we enter into a relationship we have to step back and ask ourselves, "Why do I want a boyfriend?" If your honest answer is because you're looking for someone to fulfill your desire to feel loved, you might want to think twice before entering into that relationship. God wants us to come to the point where we're so stable and secure in God's love that if His call for us was to be single now, or even for the rest of our lives, it wouldn't matter, because His love would satisfy us completely.

Single for the rest of my life? You've got to be kidding me. No, I'm not, and I want to bring up the fact that not every single girl on this earth is going to end up with a husband. It is true that God has called some people to be single for their entire lives. In this world that is so focused on sexual desires and pleasures, it might seem like a horrific thing to think about. But we can never forget that a spouse will never fulfill our every desire in life, and God must always be our central desire, and our entire security. He *has* to be enough. Remember, God *knows* the desires of our hearts, and He also knows what the best plan for our lives is in order to fulfill His ultimate purpose for our lives. I promise you, if you make it your ultimate goal in life to love God and do His will for you, you will not be disappointed.

There are other ways that we can tell whether or not we're really going into a romantic relationship with the right reasons. Taking a look at our real motives for getting into the relationship can tell a lot. If you're entering into a relationship, eagerly anticipating the fact that you'll become more popular with a certain group of people, that's probably a sign that your motives are in the wrong place. Are you dating a guy because your friends told you to? Are you dating a guy just

WHAT'S LOVE GOT TO DO WITH IT? A LOT!

because you know you're making someone else jealous? Are you dating a guy because you know you've got him wrapped around your finger and he'll give you anything you want? Again, if the answer is "yes" to any of these questions, you're probably not in the relationship for the right reason.

Just like I did with the "how far is too far" question, I'm not going to answer the question "should I date?" *for* you. I want God to answer the question for you instead. It's not in my place to give you a final verdict. Just keep in mind that God is ready and very willing to guide you in the choices that you make if you ask Him. I think it's so easy to get this idea that God couldn't care less about romance. Before I knew better I had this idea that I had to figure things out on my own, maybe with some helpful advice from my mom. Well, I learned that it's just the opposite. Although my mom *can* give me some very good advice, God can give the *best* advice. God cares a tremendous amount about our love lives. He is the ultimate creator of romance. He created marriage, he created sex, and he created us with the desire to have romantic relationships with the opposite sex. If you think God isn't "cool" enough to pick out an awesome guy that fits your perfect match of what you want in a guy, you're wrong. God is fully aware of our hearts' desires and wants to give us the most wonderful guy one day.

Which brings me to my next thought…what kind of guy are we looking for? Or more importantly, what kind of guy does God want us to look for?

Now, I know what you may be thinking: *Oh great, now she's going to suggest that I wait for some dorky Christian guy that's no fun at all.* If that's what you're thinking, I'm sorry. *Sorry for what*? I'm sorry that you haven't yet gotten the chance to meet the kind of guy that God's waiting to give you. If you have the idea in your head that any guy that *God* would pick out is going to be a boring guy who doesn't like to have any fun, get it out of your head! A true man of God isn't any of those things. And yes, God wants to give you a true man after His heart. I admit it; guys that have totally committed their entire lives to God are the minority. They may not be the easiest things to find, but they *are* out there. And they are ten times better than a rich and popular guy who doesn't know the Lord at all. I can't tell you whether or not you'll meet him in your senior year, date until after college, have three kids and live happily ever after, or if you'll go all through high school and college without ever dating a guy and then meet him when you're 23. Only God knows the big picture of our love life. The only thing we can do is to always make sure that we're following in His will. One way we can do that is by constantly asking God to clearly tell us what His will is for our dating life. God desires so much for us to ask Him to guide us in this area of our lives; He *will* come through and answer us, we just have to have hearts open to what He tells us. And we have to be willing to go through with what He's telling us and trust that it's the best thing for us. I can tell you for sure that it is. It may seem at the time like it's the *worst* possible thing for us or it might seem like God's telling us to go through with the hardest option, but in the long run we'll be *so* thankful that we listened to God's voice.

I've had to make some *really* tough decisions about guys that I really cared for. I hated to go through with the decisions but I knew that God was telling me to. Some decisions I've made haven't made sense to me or to anyone else around me. And honestly, that's the way it can go. Sometimes when God tells you something about a relationship, it's going to sound completely crazy to not only you, but also to everyone around you, which can make it all the more hard to go through with. I'm not trying to discourage you by scaring you into thinking that God's will is always going to be the most horrible thing you'll have to go through. It's not. Sometimes it's a lot harder to go through with than other times, but going through with something that we're not sure *why* we have to go through with will only increase our faith and trust in God and make us stronger in the end.

Relationships with the opposite sex are a huge part of our lives right now. But the awesome thing is that God has this amazing plan for this part of our lives and He wants to reveal that plan to us little by little as we seek after Him for direction for this area in our lives. God will *not* disappoint you with His plan—I can promise you that. I encourage you, seek God with your whole heart and place Him first in your life. Let His love fill that void in your heart and let it become *enough* for you. As you begin to allow God to become the ultimate love in your life, you'll realize that you've never experienced anything better before. Ask God to place His hand over your love story here on Earth and ask Him to give you the strength and trust to go through with what He asks of you. God will *not* let you down.

My Own Thoughts
How is God speaking to you about relationships? Is there anything you want to change? Is there anything you need to ask forgiveness for?

_____

_____

_____

– – –

WHAT ABOUT THE PAST?
How you can find freedom from past mistakes

Have you been reading this chapter all the while thinking, "It's too late. I've already messed up in this area of my life so why try to make things right again? I've ignored God over and over and He's probably given up on me." Maybe you've lost your virginity to a past boyfriend. Maybe you've given your heart away one too many times. Maybe you've never actually had sex but you've pushed the limits. Maybe you've left God out of your entire love life up to this point. I don't know your story, but I do know that God is standing right in front of you with open arms, ready to forgive you. God is the God of second chances.

God has promised to forgive us of our sins when we ask Him in 1 John 1:9, which says, "If we confess our sins he is faithful and just and will forgive us our sins and purify us from all unrighteousness." (NIV) God is the God of true freedom and He is waiting to let you live in His freedom if you come to His feet and ask Him to make you clean.

In Psalms 103:12 David speaks of God's unfailing love and forgiveness:

"As far as the east is from the west, so far has he removed our transgressions from us." What an amazing verse of freedom! After we ask God for forgiveness, our sins are long gone. Micah 7:19 says, "You will again have compassion on us; you will tread our sins underfoot and hurl all our iniquities into the depths of the sea." Again, this is such an awesome verse that speaks of God's unfailing forgiveness. God not only *tramples* our sins underneath His foot, but He hurls them into the depths of the sea; they're long gone! All three of the verses that I've mentioned make it clear that sin does not have to dwell in our hearts forever. There is freedom and there is forgiveness in God alone.

If you feel as though you've messed up even once or too many times to remember, confess every past mistake to God. Lay your hurts, your tears, and all of your emotional baggage at His feet and let Him cleanse your heart and your life. There's nothing He would rather do for you than to bring you into a life of ultimate freedom from sin living under the complete redemption of His love. Never think that you've gone too far past the point where you can be forgiven. God will forgive a hundred sins as quickly as He'll forgive one sin. *We just have to ask.*

— — —

My Own Thoughts

_____

_____

_____

_____

_____

_____

_____

Your Next Mission: Get Down on Your Knees!
It's never too early to pray for someone you don't know yet

To wrap up this chapter on relationships, I want to add one more thing that has become very important to me over the last couple of years: praying for my future spouse. When I first heard someone talk about praying for my future spouse I thought it was almost a weird idea. But I soon learned that it's one of the best things I can do to prepare for my future. You're not going to have a specific name to pray for, but God knows who you're praying for.

The point of praying for your future husband is not to pray and ask God for a specific guy that you already know, but to pray for "that guy," trusting that God knows who He is. Here are some things you might want to consider praying for your future spouse:

Pray for the choices that your future husband is making right now. Pray that your future spouse would be listening to God's voice in his life and that he would be making choices in his relationships that are pleasing to God. Ask that God would give him the strength to listen to His voice and resist the temptation that may come his way to do anything that wouldn't honor God, or anything in a relationship sense that wouldn't honor his future with you.

Pray for you future husband's relationship with his parents. This might sound like a weird one, but believe me, it's important! Your relationship with your parents can tell a lot about your temper, your ego, and even your relationship with God. In Exodus 20:12 God orders us in the Ten Commandments, "Honor your father and mother..." (NIV) If God put it in the Ten Commandments, then He obviously thinks it's pretty important. I think it's such a good sign in a guy when he has a great and loving relationship with his parents and when he doesn't think he's too "cool" to kiss him mom goodbye. Besides, there's always that saying that the way a guy treats his mom is the way he'll treat his future wife, and I'm pretty sure that saying rings true.

There is the chance that your future husband will come from a broken, battered home. His parents may have abused him or left him. Pray that if that is the case, that your future spouse will have found it in his heart to forgive them and find healing from the hurt and pain that his family life may have caused him.

Pray that God would give your husband financial wisdom. Though it may seem unimportant at the time, being wise with the finances God blesses you with can make or break a marriage. Seeing the way my dad has handled our family's savings so wisely, yet hearing so many stories of how families have sunk into debt because of a husband's gambling addiction or something related has caused me to really realize how important it is. Bringing a mountain of debt into a marriage can cause a lot of unnecessary problems.

Pray that God would give your husband a heart of contentment. Pray that your future husband would be content with wherever God chooses to put him financially and that his main goal in life would not be to always have more material possessions. Pray that his heart would instead look for fulfillment in gaining things that have eternal value and that his mind would not always be on having something bigger, better, and more expensive.

Pray that your husband's ultimate goal in life would be to seek God with his whole heart and please Him in every area of his life. If your future husband's ultimate goal in life is to please God with everything he does, it will show in your marriage. Pray that he will make this decision early on in his life and that he will put a lot of value on it.

Starting to pray for your future husband now is one of the best things you can do to prepare for your future marriage. Do you know how awesome it will be when you meet your future husband and you're able to tell him that you've been praying for him before you even met? Even if you can take the time just once a week to pray for different areas in your future mate's life, you're still making a difference in his life and one day you'll both reap the reward.

My Own Thoughts
The Top Ten Qualities I Desire in my Future Husband

1. _____
2. _____
3. _____
4. _____
5. _____
6. _____
7. _____
8. _____
9. _____
10. _____

WHAT'S LOVE GOT TO DO WITH IT? A LOT!

If you could talk to your future husband right now what would you say to him?

_____

_____

_____

_____

_____

_____

_____

_____

_____

- - -

AT THE END OF THE DAY
So this is what I've said about relationships

- The message of love that the world is sending us is false and a cheap imitation of what God really has for us.
- There's a void in each one of us that only God can fill. It's a void that we can try to fill with other loves, but we will only feel fulfilled when God's love fills the void.
- Before we enter into a romantic relationship we must completely fall in love with Christ. Falling in love with Christ takes discipline and genuine desire. We must spend

time with God and get to know His character. We're going to have to make sacrifices if we truly want to do this.

- We're told over and over to stay pure before marriage by remaining a virgin. This is only part of staying pure until marriage. We must keep our hearts pure by carefully guarding them in our relationships with the opposite sex.

- When you're trying to figure out "how far is too far," remember that God's two greatest commands were to love Him first, and then to love others as you would love yourself. Apart from setting specific physical boundaries for yourself, ask yourself if you're following these two commands when you're doing whatever you're doing.

- Before you date, let God become enough for you. Make sure that you don't enter into a romantic relationship with the wrong motives in your heart.

- God may ask you to make some hard decisions about relationships but He's the only one that can see the big picture and He's only asking you to do what will be in your best interest in the long run.

- If you've messed up in the past, there's forgiveness and redemption! All we have to do is humble ourselves before the throne of God and ask Him! He's ready and willing to make us as clean as snow.

- Pray for your future husband! It's one of the best ways to prepare for marriage and it's never too early to start.

- Remember…raise the bar.

— — —

RECOMMENDED READING

OK, I'm really going to end this chapter now, I promise. But before I do I want to tell you about some books that encouraged me in my decisions about how I handle romantic relationships. They've changed my views on a lot of things and have opened my eyes to concepts I never realized before. Even if you're not an avid reader, I encourage you to flip through at least one of these books. I guarantee you'll find something that catches your eye and makes you think twice.

Authentic Beauty, Leslie Ludy. Sisters, OR: Multnomah Publishers, Inc., 2003.

We live in a world where young women and girls are expected to be flirtatious and attractive. They're expected to wear their hearts on their sleeves and give guys what they want. The word "classy" has been replaced with "sexy." Young women are giving their bodies away hoping to find the love they have dreamed of ever since they were young girls. And not only are women throwing their bodies away, but also their hearts, throwing them into the wind waiting for the first guy that pretends to be interested.

Fortunately, Leslie Ludy has crafted a beautiful book, instructing young women and girls on how they can escape the world's trap and run after the real Prince. Leslie stresses the point that, as young women and girls, we need to fall in love with our Prince and carefully guard His Sanctuary (our hearts) before we pursue a romantic relationship. The reason that this is such a great book is that Leslie's instructions apply to every single girl out there. She discusses many possible situations and realizes that we're only human and we will make mistakes. This book offers hope and truth to every girl, no matter where she is coming from. Her instructions are full of so much truth and they're not impossible either. I highly recommend this book for every girl and woman ranging from the age of 13-70! Everyone will get something out of it.

When God Writes Your Love Story, Eric and Leslie Ludy. Sisters, OR: Multnomah Publishers, Inc., 1999.

This book encourages young people to hand their love story completely over to God and let Him be the author of every single chapter. The book lays out practical steps to do so, and by the time I was done reading it I was totally convinced that I needed to make some changes in my love life. Leslie and Eric take turns writing the chapters and the result is a book that both guys and girls will enjoy. They both use humorous but reverent references to their own lives and other stories that bring the book together into something that gives so much hope for anyone who's longing for something more than what the world has to offer when it comes to love.

Relationships: The Key to Love, Sex, and Everything Else, Dean Sherman. Seattle, WA: YWAM Publishing, 1999.

Dean Sherman's book takes on a lot of fresh new views. He discusses different things such as something he calls our "attraction gift" and in one of my favorite chapters he thoroughly explains the definitions of words that God uses in the Bible dealing with romantic relationships. The book is candid and practical and Dean Sherman does an awesome job of laying out the bare truth of it all without trying to cover anything up. After I read it I left feeling challenged and so much more informed about God's true desire for how we go about our relationships during such a crucial part of our lives.

Chapter 4

Where Moth And Rust Destroy: Where Are Your Treasures?

Matthew 6:19-21, "Do not store up for yourselves treasures on earth, where moth and rust destroy, and where thieves break in and steal. But store up for yourselves treasures in heaven, where moth and rust do not destroy, and where thieves do not break in and steal. For where your treasure is, there your heart will be also." (NIV)

YOU GOTTA GET IT…NOW!
They're telling me who, what where and when…and I wish they'd tell me why!

It's a very clever advertising market out there; the magazine ads, the TV commercials, the billboards, they've all caught my attention thousands of times. It's funny how easy it is to buy into a product just because the commercial made it look so good, or just because your favorite celebrity was seen posing with it. And oh, the world of ever so fickle trends!

As I'm writing this, the trendy thing to have is a Dooney & Bourke purse, mostly the white ones with the little initials all over in different colors. Don't know what I'm talking about? If you don't, it's probably because the trend has now ended and the world has moved on to another brand. Go figure.

Society, with the help of millions of dollars put into advertising, has been telling us who, what, where and when for as long as I can remember.

WHO has to have it? YOU do!
WHAT do I have to have? THIS!
WHERE do I get it? From THIS brand!
WHEN do I need it? NOW!

If only society would answer one more question for us: WHY? Why do we need to have a certain brand? Why do we need to have a certain product? Why do we even need it at all? It's very apparent that the world we're living in has become very materialistic. Money and possessions seem to be two of the only things we live for. We want, want, want, expecting to be happy after we've obtained the latest toy on our list, only to find that after we have it, we're still left wanting more.

I'm scared that our generation has bought into this worldly greed one too many times, and I know for a fact that materialism is holding us back from accomplishing God's plan for our lives. Materialism is a very powerful tool that Satan has been using for years on young people and I'm sorry to say that many times he's gotten the better of us. And he loves every second of it.

I think that materialism is an especially hard issue for girls to deal with. It seems as though we have so many more items and products marketed at us. And the variety is bewildering. We have to choose from belts, purses, casual shoes, dress shoes, jewelry, makeup, hair products, hair accessories, and the list goes on. The typical guy doesn't care whether or not his shoes match his outfit perfectly, whereas girls tend to care a little more, which results in having a greater variety of shoes in the closet. And then there are purses. I'm a sucker for both, shoes and purses. Shoes and purses are fun accessories, yet they still cause us girls to spend gobs of money. I'm telling you, they're traps. Oh, and don't even get me started on jewelry.

I'm in no way trying to justify a girl dealing with materialism as opposed to a guy dealing with materialism. I'm only trying to point out the fact that, as girls, I think we need to keep a closer watch over the issue. We might not think it's fair that it's a tougher thing for us to go through than guys, but guess what? Life isn't fair.

If this generation were able to find the true secret to contentment (which I'll talk about later), and pass that secret down to generations to come, the world would truly be changed. Focuses would shift, and goals would change. People would change. God wants to make some big changes in this world dealing with materialism and greed, and I think that our generation needs to get it going.

My Own Thoughts

_____

_____

_____

_____

_____

_____

ONE OF MY BIGGEST BATTLES
My ongoing battle with materialism

Remember the void inside all of us that I was talking about earlier? Often times we don't only try to fill that void with love from *people* but we also try to fill it by investing our lives in *material gain. Perhaps,* we think, *if I have a bigger, more beautiful house, a nicer car, trendier clothes, I'll be happier, and my life will be more complete.* We toil away so that we can get those things before every ounce of our happiness slips away. I've got to get them and I've got to get them now! Life is on the way as soon as I can get my hands on _____. You fill in the blank.

Materialism: It's truly been one of my biggest struggles. I've tried not to look in my closet and wish for more. I've tried not to flip through magazines and make a mental list of what I "need." I've tried not to stroll through the mall during Christmastime and let greed overcome me. Let alone that, I've tried it in the fall, spring, and summer, too. It's hard. I think we can all admit that there are times in our lives when we just wish we had *more*.

Back to school shopping has always been a big deal around my house. When we were young my mom would take my two sisters and me to Kids R Us and to the mall for some new clothes for the start of the school year. As we got older and were all in grade school, we'd take turns taking a "school shopping and dinner night" with my mom, or sometimes my dad. We would eagerly wait for our appointed night of the week to go on this exciting expedition. We'd get a new pair of pants or two, some shoes, maybe a dress, and a few shirts. Every time we'd go home we would excitedly pour out our shopping bags on the living room floor to show our lucky finds and then proceed to put on a fashion show for the rest of the family. It might sound cheesy, but I loved it!

As I got older, the school shopping would continue, only now I needed to buy two pairs of shoes. I needed jeans *and* khaki pants. I needed at least five shirts. I began to want more and more for the beginning of the school year. I mean, I can't just wear what I wore last year!

In ninth grade I entered a public school for the first time in my life and I wanted to make sure I had the right clothes, the right *stuff*. As I went through the first two years, materialism began to take its toll on my life. In my freshman and sophomore years I didn't exactly come to grips with it, but it was there. I began to acquire this selfish greed that would look at what other girls around me were wearing and make me wish that I had more, cooler clothes. I needed a pair of shoes to go with every outfit. I needed necklaces, bracelets, earrings, purses, and belts to match my outfits. I spent tons of money trying to get things that I thought would make me happier. It turned into a greed for not only things that I wore but also just things that I had in general. I would spend my paychecks getting the best accessories for my room, more makeup that I didn't wear anyways, pajama pants, T-shirts, bags, and the list goes on. But every time I'd buy something new, I'd decide that I needed something else.

When I got my driver's license my sophomore year it only got worse. Now I could drive myself to the mall anytime I wanted. Plus, I had a job that paid more than what most people my age were getting. I had money to spare, and I spent it, all the time hoping that one time I'd feel as though I finally had enough. I waited, but that time never came.

During the summer after my sophomore year I spent tons of money on clothes for the next school year. I took countless trips to the mall, looking for the right outfits, shoes, etc. My mind was always on what I needed to buy. I'd make lists of what clothes I "needed" to get before school started over and over. My materialistic nature was at its peak while during a missions trip with my youth group. I even used paper from my prayer journal to make a list of things I needed to get when I went back home. I went back to my journal to see if I could find the list but I think I ripped it out and threw it away from embarrassment at such a stupid thing. And what do you think I did the night after I got home from my missions trip? I went shopping. By myself. And it left me unfulfilled. Again.

It was during those times that I began to realize the fact that while I was obtaining so many different things, all of my efforts to find happiness were in vain. Ashamed, I began to realize how much effort, how much money and time I had put into material gain. And although I continued to have a relationship with God (still steady and stable) I had replaced a majority of my thoughts and energies on the next thing I could get my hands on, instead of filling my mind with all of God's wonderful blessings, and instead of really taking as much time as I needed to get to know Him more so that I could become the girl that He wanted me to become. I wasn't growing in my relationship with God at the pace God wanted. I was stuck in a worldly trap, holding myself back from a life of contentment.

During my junior year, God really began to speak to me about my materialistic heart. I became very aware that it was something that needed to immediately change in my life. On April 18 of my junior year, I wrote in my journal:

I'm slowly discovering that others will always seem to have more than me. I'll never have all of my wants…someone will always have a nicer car, cuter clothes, more clothes, a cooler room. I'll never be totally satisfied. But yet, there is hope. There is complete fulfillment. There is contentment. There is peace. There is joy. There is Jesus. And He is enough.

God was doing a much-needed work in my life dealing with materialism. Unfortunately, I'm unable to say that I've got it perfect now. I don't. I still struggle with it every day. But God continuously makes it clear to me that materialism is a part of my life that I need to change. It's a tough battle, but to win this battle is worth everything I have to get the victory. I want to win. I need to win.

– – –

Where's Your Treasure?
Are you sure it's not going to be destroyed?

In the verse that was quoted at the beginning of the chapter, from Matthew 6:19-21, God is telling us that He wants us to take a look at our lives and determine where we're storing our "treasures." He reminds us that this world is not completely secure and that there's no guarantee our possessions will last while we're living. They could be stolen. They could be destroyed by a natural disaster. They could simply grow old and rust. The basic point: earthly possessions will one day hold no value.

I was thinking about something that happened in my community this past winter. In my quaint, secure little town, fire brought us an awful tragedy. The entire house of a girl I work with burnt down. Everything was gone; family scrapbooks, mementos, clothing, books, furniture; the destruction was massive.

I had to ask myself: What if that was to happen to my family? What if my entire closet burnt to ashes? What if my bed, my big comfy chair, and my shelves of picture frames were all destroyed?

God knew very well that natural disasters and other forms of destruction were going to take place on earth. It's part of living in an imperfect world. That is why he warned us: *Store up treasures in heaven! Don't spend your life storing up things on Earth that can, and eventually will, so easily pass away. Invest your time in making eternal deposits!*

We put so much value into the things that we can see, the things that we can touch; the things that society defines us by. So we store up as much as we can. But God tells us to do the opposite. Store up things that really matter! Every time you show kindness and compassion to someone: a treasure in heaven. Every time you show extra patience to someone undeserving: a treasure in heaven. Every time you do a random act of kindness to a stranger out of the love in your heart: a treasure in heaven. Every time you cheerfully place an offering in the basket at church: a treasure in heaven. These are the treasures that life is about! These are the treasures that will never rust away! They store up in heaven and one day God will reward us for them. We're told in Matthew 16:27, NIV note "For the Son of Man is going to come…and then he will reward each person according to what he has done." God's not going to care if you had a shiny, black Jaguar. He's not going to care how big your house was or how many cruises you went on. God is going to care about the treasures you stored up in His kingdom. 1 Timothy 6:18-19 says, "Tell them to go after God…to do good, to be rich in helping others, to be extravagantly generous. If they do that, they'll build a treasury that will last, gaining life that is truly life." (Msg)

So where have you been storing your treasures? Are they piling up in your bedroom creating a mountain of useless junk? Are they bulging out of your closet? Are they sitting outside in the driveway with the windows down? Are you creating a lasting treasury in heaven?

I know I've been storing too many "treasures" in my closet lately and God has been gently reminding me of the things that really matter. Every time I read the passage in Matthew 6 when God's teaching about worry, my heart becomes humbled, especially when I read what God says about clothes. Matthew 6:28 (Msg) says, "All this time and money wasted on fashion—do you think it makes that much difference? Instead of looking at the fashions, walk out into the fields and look at the wildflowers. They never primp or shop, but have you ever seen color and design quite like it? The ten best-dressed men and women in the country look shabby alongside them." Having the best and the most clothes in my closet is not something God counts as an eternal treasure and I find myself having to remind myself of that all the time. Clothing, along with so many other things, is counted as a treasure here on earth, but it ends there. God doesn't care how fashionable my clothes are and how well my shoes match.

God actually brings up the subject of materialism a lot in the Bible, not just in Matthew 6. He doesn't use the exact words, but He talks a lot about our greedy attitudes, our love for money, and so on. If we take some time to look at what His word says about it all, we'll find that the world's focus on money is totally opposite of what God wants us to focus on.

You've Got to Choose Your Master
Be careful whom you bow down to...

1 John 2:15-17, "Don't love the world's ways. Don't love the world's goods. Love of the world squeezes out love for the Father. Practically everything that goes on in the world – wanting your own way, wanting everything for yourself, wanting to appear important – has nothing to do with the Father. It just isolates you from him. The world and all its wanting, wanting, wanting is on the way out—but whoever does what God wants is set for eternity." (Msg)

I don't think it's a coincidence how many times God addresses money and greed in the Bible. I think that He knew all along what a covetous and selfish world we'd one day inhabit. When I was looking at different verses addressing the topic I noticed the same tone in each verse and I noticed a pattern in what was being said. Looking at the pattern I think it makes it easier to determine what God has in mind for this area in our lives and I also think it reveals a lot about the nature of God.

I was talking earlier about a passage in Matthew 6. God was talking about worrying. I think a lot of times when we hear the word "worry" we think of situations like worrying for a test in school, worrying for our safety in a dangerous situation, or worrying about a loved one's health. But have you ever thought of money when you think about worrying? I don't think we even always realize it, but money and worry actually go hand in hand a lot. Some people worry about not having enough money to pay the bills. Of course, wanting to pay the bills would never be seen as materialism. But have you ever worried about not being "cool" enough, and as a result you worried about your possessions? Did you worry that your clothes weren't cool enough or that people would make fun of your beatup car? Did you worry about what people would think about the size of your house or how nice it was inside?

I think that worry about these things is so common among everyone, especially at this age, when the pressures of our society are so tight around us and become such a driving force in our lives. I know God recognized this worry in humans because He sees into our hearts. God knew that in turn those senseless little worries would create a selfish greed in our hearts to have things that were newer, more in fashion, bigger, etc. It says in 1 Chronicles 28:9, "...for the Lord searches every heart and understands every motive behind the thoughts..." (NIV) Is greed ever a secret motive behind our worries? I have no doubt that it is. Yet, even if we think it's a secret, it's no secret to God. He can see everything that goes on inside our hearts. Why do you think that when Jesus was talking about the subject of worry one of his main focuses was on worrying about what you were dressed in? He knew that a key source of greed in our lives started out with worry and He wanted to provide a way out for us. He wanted to let us know that our worry could be stopped in its tracks before it turned into greed.

The Bible says, "What I'm trying to get you to do here is relax, to not be so preoccupied with *getting*, so you can respond to God's giving. People who don't know God and the way He works fuss over these things, but you know both God and how he works. Steep your life in God-reality, God-initiative, God-provisions. Don't worry about missing out. You'll find all your everyday human concerns will be met. Give your entire attention to what God is doing right now..." (Matthew 6:31-34a, Msg)

The Bible is simply saying to us: relax. Look to God. Look at what God is doing in your life! Stop worrying about the clothes on your back! Stop worrying about your possessions, period. Compared to what God is doing, they simply don't matter. Come see how He provides. And come see that what He provides is enough for this short-lived life! This is not your eternal home!

In Hebrews 13:5 I found the same message: "Don't be obsessed with getting more material things. Be relaxed with what you have. Since God assured us, 'I'll never let you down, never walk off and leave you,' we can boldly quote, God is there, ready to help; I'm fearless no matter what. Who or what can get me?" (Msg)

Relax. Stop obsessing over those jeans you want. Stop thinking every second about the clothes you want to buy before school starts. Stop wishing you had another pair of shoes, a cooler cell phone, and a nicer car. Focus on God!

I can't believe how much God uses these verses to speak to me. I know there have been many times in my life where I needed to read these verses and hear God say, "Tessa Sean Hershberger! Relax!"

Several times I did hear this voice. A few times I would hear a speaker speaking on something along the lines of contentment, materialism, etc. and I would hear God's voice whispering to my heart. Unfortunately, I didn't always listen. I knew inside my heart that I needed so badly to listen, yet my selfish human nature took over the work that God was trying to do in my heart and I found myself turning away and continuing to focus on material gain.

I soon discovered the consequences. My greedy thoughts began to interrupt the time I was spending with God and I would get easily distracted. My mind would drift off into shopping land and I'd think about what I'd find at the mall the next day. It really put a dent into my quiet times with God because I wasn't totally focusing on what I was reading in His word and what He was trying to tell me. As a result of not very effective quiet times, areas of my relationship with God began to dwindle and I found that I started to feel farther away from God.

Money was becoming the master of my heart and my thoughts, the very thing that God cautions us about in Matthew 6:24. God tells us plainly, "No one can serve two masters. Either he will hate the one and love the other, or he will be devoted to one and despise the other. You cannot serve both God and Money." (NIV.)

Often times I would think about this verse. But I don't hate God! I love God with all my heart! OK, so maybe I like money, but I'd never, ever hate God. I don't despise Him either! And I'm usually pretty devoted to God. It never worked then to try and justify myself according to this verse and it never will. God says it plain and simple: It's either Me or money. Pick one. It's a truly black and white situation.

It shouldn't be hard to pick one and the best choice is obvious to me: God, of course! But why is it so hard to completely devote my entire life to Him and make Him, instead of earthly possessions, my heart's true focus? It's because (I've said it twice before now) the world does not flow in the same way as God! The world around us doesn't understand and it never will unless we begin to set a new standard!

In Matthew 19 we find the story of a rich young man who came to Jesus and asked Him what he should do to get eternal life. After telling Jesus that he already obeys the commandments, he asks Jesus, is there anything else I need? Jesus tells him, "Sell your possessions and give to the poor, and you will have treasure in heaven. Then come, follow me." (Matthew 19:21.) It goes on to say, "When the young man heard this, he went away sad, because he had great wealth. Then Jesus said to his disciples, 'I tell you the truth, it is hard for a rich man to enter the kingdom of heaven'." (Matthew 19:22-23, NIV) Why is it so hard for us to "sell everything" and follow God? Why is it so hard to leave a life of wealth behind to walk in the footsteps of the very God that saved our souls from an eternal life of torture?

Wait. Does this verse mean I have to give everything I have to goodwill and never buy a new outfit again while living on the streets of the city? Does this mean that a rich person cannot go to Heaven? No. God does not desire for us all to live in poverty and wind up homeless on the streets. A person with money in the bank will not automatically go to hell, and it's not a sin to be financially secure (although there's a pretty awesome alternative that I'm going to talk about later). However, it is a sin when money gets in the way of our following Jesus with our entire heart, soul, and mind. It's a sin when money is our main goal in life and we sit around letting our thoughts drift off to think about how much we're going to earn. What about the rich man getting into heaven? God says it's hard for a rich man to enter into the kingdom of heaven because, in reality, great riches lead to a life of temporary happiness that makes a person think that life is fine without God. Wealth can so easily bring people short-term security and defense against loneliness and a longing for God's love in their life.

That is why we have to be so, so careful as to how we handle our money as Christians. We must keep close watch that money never becomes a master in our life and that our thoughts are always on the right page with God.

God's not calling us to live in rags, but He is calling us to be willing to live in rags if that is what it takes to follow Him. God is not calling us to give all of our furniture to the poor and eat dinner on the floor, but He is calling for us to be willing to sell our house and leave for the mission field if

He calls us to it. No, God's call will never be any more than we can take. But His call will always be: "Follow Me. Relax. Stop worrying about what you can gain and start looking heavenward to what I'm doing in your life and the world around you."

God's not so much concerned about money as an object. We need it to provide for our needs. In this country you basically need money if you want to just survive. God is concerned about how we handle money here on Earth and how it affects our relationship with Him. The second there's even a hint of money becoming our master over Himself, that's when God becomes concerned. He made it plain and clear to us in His word through a number of scriptures: We are to be content with what we have and devote ourselves to Him. So does this mean I can never go out and buy a new shirt? Does this mean God never wants us to have nice things? Does this mean we can never have a girls' night out shopping trip? No, I don't believe so. I do believe that there are ways to determine whether or not we're following God's rule of contentment in our lives. I think we have to dig into our motives, the true reflections of our heart, to see what really lies beneath. Just a few questions you could ask yourself:

- Do I worry constantly, daily, or at all about what people think of my possessions (clothes, car, house, etc.)?
- Do my thoughts often wander off into the things that I want to buy?
- Do I have thoughts in my head that if I could only buy a certain thing then life would finally be complete and I would be accepted and happy?
- When I'm spending time with God, do my thoughts ever turn into a mental list of the things that I need or just want to buy?

- Has a quest for material gain gotten in the way of the time I spend with God? (Example: going to the mall every day instead of spending time with God).
- Do I often look at other people and wish I had the things they had and instantly feel that my possessions are not good enough?
- Do I purposely spend too much time at a job so that I can earn extra money to buy more clothes, electronic "toys," etc. that I don't really need?

So what were your answers to the questions? Honestly, there have been different times in my life when I could have probably answered yes to all of those questions. Contentment has not yet been a permanent victory for me and I'm learning more each day to grasp it. I know God has been trying to reveal it to me.

But what is the true secret to contentment and what kind of contentment is God calling us to? Is God even asking something possible of us when He calls us to be content in a world where material gain rules the lives of so many? Of course! God wouldn't ask us to be content if He wasn't ready to help us attain that part of His nature and if it wasn't something that we as humans could accomplish.

Paul claimed to have discovered the secret to contentment and he wrote about it in Philippians. In Philippians 4:11-13 Paul writes,

> "Actually, I don't have a sense of needing anything personally. I've learned by now to be quite content whatever my circumstances. I'm just as happy with little as with much, with much as with little. I've found the recipe for being happy whether full or

> **hungry, hands full or hands empty. Whatever I have, wherever I am, I can make it through anything in the One who makes me who I am."** *(Msg)*

Wow. I think Paul really had the hang of it. His words are so bold and straightforward, yet I know they were genuine because Paul did not always have life handed to him on a platter. He very much knew what it meant to be in need. In 2nd Corinthians 11:27 he says, "…I have known hunger and thirst and have often gone without food; I have been cold and naked." (NIV) Paul really meant what he said. He was not some rich man sitting on a royal throne with servants by his side feeding him grapes saying, "Ha! Now this is the life! Yep, I'm content! Someone fetch me my slippers!" No, Paul was a man that gave his life to serve Christ and he truly knew what it meant to go without. Yet, as he writes, his bare minimum needs don't even seem to matter much and he lets us know that he's content whether he's got a shirt on his back or not.

What is Paul's secret recipe? In a world that beat him down and left him with empty hands, where did he find such a fulfillment in life? How did he reach the point where he no longer cared what he had to gain but the only thing he cared about was accomplishing God's plan for his life and reaching the lost?

> **He finally realized who he was living for. He finally realized who was living in him. He finally realized the source of each passing breath. Paul finally realized that every single thing he had to gain on this earth worth anything at all came through Christ and Christ alone. Only Christ mattered!**

To be truly content we must fall down on our knees before the throne of the Father and totally relinquish every hope of finding a life worth living through material possessions. We must realize that we live because of what Christ did for us on the cross; we have something eternal through a loving Savior that gives us every ounce of strength we need to live. We must cling to the very fact that our lives are from the one, true, living God and that as long as our eyes are constantly upon His love and beauty, nothing else in this world should matter.

I think that one of the reasons that even Christians have such a hard time being content is because we often fail to fully realize Who Christ is and what He's given us. We believe in His grace but we fall short of realizing the intensity of it and the complete transformation that it makes in our future after we leave earth. Finally, we fail to comprehend the immensity of God's love and just how sufficient it really is. We forget that when Jesus died on the cross for our sins, He gave us the one and only thing we really needed in life: eternal life after we die. After we accept that gift, we enter into His family and become His children. And God supplies everything His children need.

Sometimes on earth it may seem as though God gave us the wrong things or as though He didn't give us enough. At that point we try to fix the "problem" by trying to collect everything we think God forgot to give us: clothes, cars, houses, etc. Other times we simply don't fully realize that after we've accepted Christ into our lives we already have everything we need, so we spend our little precious time on earth looking for things to give us a purpose, when in reality, God has a much bigger and much more meaningful purpose for us to fulfill. If only we'd realize what Paul realized.

— — —

WHERE MOTH AND RUST DESTROY: WHERE ARE YOUR TREASURES?

My Own Thoughts
Where have you been storing your treasure? Who has been your master: God or money?

_____

_____

_____

_____

_____

_____

_____

_____

A PICTURE IN MY MIND

1 Timothy 6:6, "But godliness with contentment is great gain." (NIV)

Two summers ago my youth group took a life-changing missions trip to Haiti. Months before we left I was very eagerly awaiting the trip because I knew it would be an awesome experience, something totally out of the ordinary. I knew that the Haitians were a needy people and that our going there would supply them with many things they were in need of.

As I packed my bags before the long-awaited trip, I mostly packed things that I could leave there. Before the trip I had gone to the thrift store to stock up on t-shirts and gym shorts that I could take along with me to wear and give away after I was done. I also found a few pieces of old clothing in my closet that I wanted to give away. So, I was pretty much expecting to return home empty-handed. I ended up coming home with a lot more than an empty suitcase. I came home with a whole new knowledge of what it means to literally have nothing.

When we arrived in Haiti we could immediately see the poverty that would surround us for the next five days. As we rode from the Haitian airport on the dirty streets, scrunched in the backs of open trucks, either on wooden benches or standing, we got an authentic glimpse of the images we had so many times seen on TV, from various commercials asking for money for deprived and starving children. We went on to learn that we weren't even in the poorest part of the country; it was way worse elsewhere.

There were already three little girls awaiting us at the mission house if I remember right. Dressed in dirty and worn dresses they were so excited to see us. Later we were joined by a whole group of children from the village. Most of them were barefoot, and if they had shoes they were old and ragged. Clothing was soiled and had the hand-me-down look. The adults that came and visited were perhaps a little cleaner than the children, but the clothes were not nice as we'd say in America. These people were poor. Yet, if you couldn't tell a rag from a crisp white button-down, you wouldn't even know. Their faces were not dragging on the ground. They didn't walk around frowning. They had life and energy and joy! They excitedly walked us down the street and graciously invited us into their homes, their faces full of pride as we walked through small, cramped "rooms" with whatever possessions they had packed together.

As I walked through one of the houses I couldn't believe my eyes. To these people, we were practically millionaires! They had nothing, yet they were full of Christ's love and joy and hospitality. I'm a selfish American, I thought. I have so much compared to these people! My house would be a mansion to them and my meals lavish and huge. I am a selfish American.

On the last full day we were there, a Sunday, we attended the church service. We packed into a small, humid building with only a few ceiling fans to cool our sweaty brows in the ninety degree weather. It was hot. But let me tell you–the Haitians were excited to be praising God! It didn't matter what they were wearing compared to us. It didn't matter what building they were in. Worshiping God mattered. These Haitians had discovered the secret to contentment. We sat there, amazed at the jubilant atmosphere, full of energy and vibrant passion for God in that hot and stuffy room of white wooden benches. These Haitians have experienced God's love and they truly realize that God's love is sufficient. They truly realize that God is their supplier and that God is all they need. Lord, let us be like the Haitians!

We boarded the plane to return to America, sad to leave the Haitians, and full of a whole new realization of what it meant to truly be in need. We went through customs and baggage claim and as soon as we boarded the big, comfy, air-conditioned bus to drive back to Sarasota where we would spend a few days at the beach, I remember my very thoughts. Luxury. We passed buildings and fast food restaurants and I thought to myself, We truly live in luxury compared to the millions of people around the world, Haiti included, living in sheer poverty. Lord, might I be content for the rest of my life. May I never complain about the clothes in my closet again. Might I be more generous with what I have. Might I never ever forget the sights that I saw in Haiti. Please, Lord, let them remain near to my heart for the rest of my life.

– – –

God's Greater Calling
It takes more than being content

1 Timothy 6:7-8, "Since we entered the world penniless and will leave it penniless, if we have bread on the table and shoes on our feet, that's enough." (Msg)

Have you found the secret to being content? Have you laid down your possessions before God and allowed Him to become your Master? Have you put your devotion into storing up treasures in heaven rather than on earth? Have you realized Who you were living for and what really matters in life? Now then, are you ready to give more? Are you willing to raise the bar even higher?

In the past year God has not only spoken to me about being content with what I have but He's also revealed to me something else: sacrificial living. While I do believe that contentment is a very huge goal that my generation needs to work towards in order to fulfill God's calling, I also believe that contentment is not the end of it, but only a point that must be reached before we strive towards God's next task for us.

I'm looking around my house right now. It's a nice house. It's not a mansion, but it's not small. If you were to go look in my bedroom you'd see a nice-sized room, painted yellow. There's a big, round comfy chair, a bed, a dresser, big shelves, a phone, and two closets. (I only use one closet and the other closet holds miscellaneous items that my mom can't store anywhere else.) If you opened up my closet and drawers you'd find a lot of clothes, more clothes than I really need. In the end, you'd probably define me as well off. If you were to visit the rest of the houses in my town you'd probably say the same thing for most of them. We live comfortably and have more than enough. Some houses have big screen TVs and huge entertainment systems. In some driveways there are expensive sports cars. Some houses have big decks and swimming pools.

Now, if I were to take you past the cornfields and into the streets of the inner city, you might find something different. If you looked around, you'd find smaller, older, more beatup houses. If you went inside you might find less belongings. If you went inside the apartment in the inner city where a family very dear to me lives you'd find no big comfy couches to sit on. You'd find no oak desks with computers, and you'd find no entertainment systems. You wouldn't even find a washer and dryer, or a dishwasher.

Two entirely different environments, one having more, one having less. I want you to place yourself in the shoes of a person living in my part of town. You've got everything you need to survive, and more. You're comfortable. Now, I'll put myself in the shoes of someone coming from the beatup inner city with almost nothing but the bare minimum to survive in this world . Somehow, we end up at the same church service on Sunday morning, and we even end up sitting in the same pew. As the offering baskets make their way towards us, your parents get out their checkbook and write a check for two hundred and fifty dollars, which they give every week. It doesn't hurt their income. In fact, it hardly puts a glitch in it. Your family still has plenty, more than plenty even. As you pass the offering basket to my family, we surprisingly give a check for the same amount, even though we can hardly afford it on my parents' low incomes. Of course, we could have put it into savings to save up for another car so that my mom and dad didn't have to share one. We could have saved it to buy some better clothes for the upcoming school year so we didn't have to shop at Goodwill. We opted instead to give it to the church. After church we'll have turkey and cheese sandwiches instead of going out to a restaurant, which we only do once a month.

This is not a real scenario, neither am I saying that less fortunate people always give more than they have and very fortunate people give less than they could. I simply wanted to give a more modern-day illustration of a small story found in the Bible. It only takes four small verses to give a powerful message and to portray a picture for us to emulate in our everyday lives, yet we often look past it. It's found in Luke 21:1-4:

"Just then he [Jesus] looked up and saw the rich people dropping offerings in the collection plate. Then he saw a poor widow put in two pennies. He said, 'The plain truth is that this widow has given by far the largest offering today. All these others made offerings that they'll never miss; she gave extravagantly what she couldn't afford – she gave her all!'" (Msg)

Sacrificial living at its greatest—give more than you can afford, all for giving glory to Christ to further His kingdom. The rich men in the story gave less than they could truly afford. The widow gave more than she could truly afford. She gave her all, and she gave it to the foundation that she knew would bring glory to God—the church. She literally put her life into God's hands when she gave those two pennies; her heart was willing and generous, even when the cost was huge.

Are we giving our all, more than we can afford to give? I strongly believe that our generation has become too "comfortable." We live in comfort, depend on our comfort, and dare not wander into the unknown land of the unfamiliar. When we give, if we give at all, we give "comfortably." Comfort can be a dangerous thing. Comfort can easily block us from having a greater faith in God, and a lack of trust that He'll give us every single thing we need to fulfill His purpose in our lives. When we live in comfort, we don't have to *depend* on anything because we already know we have it.

I know that living in my comfort zone is something I struggle with. When I came home from Haiti, it was as though I breathed a sigh of relief and said: "That was a true eye-opener and I'm really going to be content now. But boy am I glad I don't have to live in the midst of that poverty one more day." I was happy to go back to getting a ten-minute warm shower. I was happy to go back to my nice town. I was happy to go back to my life. A comfort zone.

What if we were to step out of our comfort zones and live life a little differently, a little *dependently*, instead of, *independently*? What if we were to start making a few sacrifices every now and then so that we could give more to God? I have such a strong belief that so many Christians are not living sacrificially and giving their all to God, and I'm talking about myself as well. Why do some church budgets suffer and others seem to thrive all the time? I believe that it is not a matter of what's available, but it's a matter of *how much we're willing to give, how much we're willing to depend on God for everyday provision and fulfillment.* If we were to sacrifice going out to eat twice a month, there'd be more for God's use. If we were to sacrifice getting that new pair of shoes we don't really need, there would be more for God's use. If we were to sacrifice even some of the money we spent on Christmas presents, there would be more for God's use. It takes God's discipline to be content, but it takes even more to live sacrificially, and I believe that God is calling our generation to go a step further, to take a leap of faith and see what can happen when we give our all.

Can we put back those three magazines every month that we don't really need? Better yet, can we use those ten dollars to glorify God? Can we put back that adorable pink leather bag when we have ten other purses that work just fine? Will we use that money instead *to glorify God*? To glorify God. To put it simply, to put everything into one little "concept." Here it is: **Our money is to be used to glorify God, and instead of creating a wall of comfort within us, it is to be used to make us all the more dependent on God as a result of giving our all for God's glory and purpose**.

> *1 Timothy 6:18-19, "Tell those rich in this world's wealth to quit being so full of themselves and so obsessed with money, which is here today and gone tomorrow. Tell them to go after God, who piles on all the riches we could ever manage—to do good, to be rich in helping others, to be extravagantly generous. If they do that, they'll build a treasury that will last, gaining life that is truly life." (Msg)*

Store up treasures in heaven, learn to be content with everything God has blessed you with, practice living sacrificially, use your money to give glory to God, and gain the life that is *truly* life—the life God wants you to live.

— — —

LOOKING IT OVER
A time to look at your own habits

Are you ready to take a long, hard look at your life? If you're ready to be honest and you want to make some changes in your life dealing with money, possessions, contentment, etc., don't wait another second. If God has spoken to your heart about something in this last chapter, write it down, and tell God your every thought. Ask Him to reveal to you things you need to change in this area in your life, and ask Him to give you the discipline to be content, and the faith to live sacrificially for God.

Write down what God reveals to you and write down your own thoughts. If your true heart's desire is to be more content, write down things that you think will help you achieve this. Does looking at a certain catalog trigger inner greed? Do you take too many pointless trips to the mall and end up leaving wishing you had things you didn't? If the answer was "yes" to either one, ask God to give you the discipline to avoid them. Instead, spend some of your time doing something for those who are needy, or think about all that you do have instead of the things you don't have.

God is so ready to jump in and guide you through this area in your life, and no matter how unpopular and hard it may be, letting God rule over your money and possessions is completely rewarding. And if we can show the world that, some great changes will begin to show up. Let's remember Who we're living for.

— — —

My Own Thoughts

_____
_____
_____
_____
_____

— — —

Wrapping it all up
Points on Possessions

- The world is sending us a message of materialism and a spirit of greed has captured our generation.
- God commands us to store up our treasures in heaven instead of storing up treasures here on earth that will eventually be destroyed. Treasures in heaven are the ones that will truly last—and they come with the best reward, too!
- Money is mentioned in the Bible numerous times because it's a subject that God didn't want us to ignore. God is waiting for us to choose between serving Him and serving money, and we must choose one. We can't try to serve them both while still fulfilling God's ultimate plan for our life.
- We've got to invest in the secret of contentment by realizing Who we're living for and that the goal is to bring God glory with our money. Contentment takes a lot of discipline—but God is waiting to help.
- Living sacrificially will allow us to develop the necessary faith and trust that God is able to fulfill us in every way we need.
- Living sacrificially can develop a generosity towards the church that will go on to further God's kingdom—what an awesome way to invest in God's plan!
- It's all about glorifying God.
- Remember…raise the bar.

- - -

Chapter 5

Who's That In The Mirror?
The False Image We've Formed

Psalms 45:11, "The King is enthralled by your beauty…" (NIV)

WHAT DO YOU BELIEVE?
What's your own take on yourself?
Is it the same as God's?

You are beautiful and lovely,
Worth more than a million diamonds

God is amazed by your beauty,
You were specially handcrafted by Him

There is a strong woman of God deep in your heart
That God is waiting for you to discover
Pure, lovely, accepted, and sealed with approval

God's love for you goes deeper than the ocean
And higher than the highest mountain
It stretches wider than the sky
It is infinite beyond your imagination

CONFESSIONS OF A GIRL

You are loved more than you know
You are worth more than you know
You are exquisite, priceless, and unique

You are God's daughter
Made in His very image, and precious in His sight

You are beautiful and lovely
Worth more than a million diamonds

Do you believe those words about yourself? Do they speak truth to you, or do you only wish you could believe them? Have you wanted to believe them for some time but gave up? If you were to go look at yourself in the mirror would you be able to recite those words to yourself and trust that God was up in heaven smiling and nodding as you painted yourself a picture of His thoughts for you?

I want you to do something. Right now, go into your room or the bathroom and look at a full-length mirror. Stare at yourself for five minutes and write down ten adjectives and phrases that come to your mind describing your physical self. Write down every single thing that you think of, good or bad, positive or negative:

1. _____
2. _____
3. _____
4. _____
5. _____
6. _____
7. _____

WHO'S THAT IN THE MIRROR? THE FALSE IMAGE WE'VE FORMED

8. _____
9. _____
10. _____

So what did you write down? *Fat? Ugly? Pretty? Too much hair? Hair too frizzy? Boobs too small? Nose too big? Lanky? Good looking? Blah?* Kudos to you if everything on the list was something positive. For most of us though, our lists were probably mostly negative things that we'd change in an instant if we could.

Now step back from looking at your physical self and just look at yourself in general, the person you are as a whole. Write down ten adjectives that you think other people would use to describe you:

1. _____
2. _____
3. _____
4. _____
5. _____
6. _____
7. _____
8. _____
9. _____
10. _____

So were those words positive or negative? *Funny? Shy? Boring? Loud? Fun? Tall? Dorky? Beautiful?* I hope that most of them were positive, but don't worry; I wasn't expecting them all to be. Don't get me wrong, it's not that I don't think that people could come up with ten good things to say about you. I said that only because I know where it's coming from: you. And in this generation, we tend to often have the wrong idea of who we are. We build a false self image and we give in to all the lies that Satan throws out at us about our appearances, our personalities, our abilities, and so on.

If there's something that I've struggled the most with over the years I would have to say that it would be my self-image. I've twisted it around, I've built it around the wrong things, and I've pushed away the truth of what God says about it too many times to count.

I also have to say that self-image is a huge problem in our generation that needs to be fixed in order to follow God's truth. Not only have we given in to the lies about our self-image but we've become obsessed with it, trying to make it perfect in every single way. We've fallen into a trap of perfectionism; we want it, and we try to tell ourselves that we absolutely need it in order to survive. And if anyone realizes how much we're going after perfectionism and a perfect self-image, it's Satan. He has, very powerfully, used society to tell us who we should be, how we should look, what we should achieve, where we should stand on the social scale, etc. We've forgotten the principles of truth that God has laid out for us and not only have we listened to the Enemy but we've counted his words as truth.

Many times I've looked in the mirror in disgust and have just hated what I saw. Other times I've thought about my personality and have just hated myself. Too many times to count I've based my self-image on what I have, what I do, and who I hang out with. And God shed a tear every single time it happened. It broke His heart that I ignored His promises and chose to believe the ultimate Enemy. *Tessa! Don't you know who you are, who I made you? I formed you! You're my child! I love you!* Yet, I went on listening to the Devil, carelessly destroying my knowledge of the truth. It started when I was only a child.

- - -

When I was about seven or eight years old, my dad would take me out for donuts every Saturday morning. Chocolate cream sticks were my favorite, those or the powdered sugar donuts that created a little white cloud of a mess around my mouth and all over my hands. And it was just my dad and I. I have two other sisters, but they didn't get to come along. This was a time for just me and my dad to be together, just the two of us.

Every Saturday we'd sit at the little table and almost every Saturday I'd say, "Dad, I hate my hair! It's so ugly!" Well, back then it *was* pretty much a big mess of frizz on top of my head (and some days it still is), but everyone else saw it as these beautiful natural curls that would cost "so much money at the salon." To me they were just awful and made me ugly.

My dad, after all my complaining, being the best dad in the world that he is, would try to convince me over and over that my hair was beautiful and that I was perfect the way I was. I still hated it. And so began my long childhood battle with my big head of thick, brown natural curls.

I continued to fight with my hair and continued to complain about it, cry about it, and whine about it. My mom and I look back and laugh at a night that we were sitting in her bathroom and I had had it up to the sky with my hair. I cried out to my mom, "Mom! I *just* HATE my hair! When I put it back in a ponytail it looks like a bunch of noodles coming out of my head on the sides!" My mom of course tried to encourage and console me but I'm sure that she was cracking up inside. That night was only one of many that I looked in the mirror and decided to hate the reflection and wish for iron straight hair like most of my friends had.

– – –

The lies concerning my self-image had caught me at a young age. *You're not pretty enough. You need to look different. Your hair is so ugly!* And even though I eventually came to appreciate my curls (on most days!), the lies didn't stop. They only began to multiply into more lies: *You're not skinny enough! You're not athletic enough! You're not popular enough!* The fight only got harder, that battle only became more complicated, and the truth floated away from my heart.

That is the way it goes with so many other girls today. They're caught in the web before they can even determine what's making them stick to it. And by the time they are able to determine that the Enemy has created a foothold in their lives through the rest of society, the media, etc., they're already in too deep. They've already believed too many lies and they've built everything around a false truth. But that's how Satan works. He loves to get a hold of us while we're vulnerable and innocent. Why would he go for someone who already knew they were created in God's image? Why would he go after someone with that kind of assurance and security? He wants the ones that aren't sure, the one's that are questioning, the one's that are about to break.

So how does Satan get a hold of us? He uses the world around us to tell us lies and to catch us in deadly traps that give us false images of ourselves. He uses just about every form of media: TV, movies, magazines, newspapers, etc. He uses our own friends, he uses some of our parents, he uses our teachers, and so on. We ask, "Who am I?" And the world tells us, "This is who you are, but this is who you need to be." The images the world gives us are wrong–both, the image of who we are and the image of who we need to be.

It's time for our generation to realize who we *really* are and stop listening to the world as it continuously tells us who to be and how we should see ourselves. **We need to look in the mirror and see the truth, and the only way we can do that is if we pinpoint the lies that Satan is telling us and exchange them for the truths that God has placed in His word**. Now, let's take a look at what the world has been telling us and see how different it is from what God has said about us from the very beginning…

– – –

My Own Thoughts

_____

_____

_____

_____

_____

_____

_____

How has the world been altering your self-image? Do you think that God would agree with what your wrote in the spaces above about yourself? Why or why not?

THE FIVE DEADLY TRAPS OF SATAN
*Pinpointing five ways in which Satan has lied to us...
have you been listening to him?*

*1 Peter 5:8, "Be self-controlled and alert. Your enemy the
devil prowls around like a roaring lion looking for
someone to devour." (NIV)*

As I grew up and began to leave my childhood and entered young adulthood, it was very evident that Satan's lies about my self-image were becoming more and more destructive in my life. Deep down inside I think I knew all along that I was listening to Satan's lies, but it had become a routine for me, something I just did.

Last year, one of my seventh grade teachers, whom all us girls loved very dearly, came into my youth group to speak to us. When Mrs. Landis came, I was at the point in my life where I was pretty aware that I was listening to a bunch of falsehoods about myself, yet I was still being held under by the world, unable to escape the poor self-image that rose to the surface of my mind constantly.

So, what do you think she talked about that night? Self-image. As soon as she passed out the outline sheet on what she would be talking about I thought, *all right Tessa, you really don't have an excuse now*! By the time she was done speaking I could have sat in my seat and cried. I was on the verge of doing so. I know at that time that God was really beginning to speak to my heart. Everything she said had spoken directly to my heart and had applied to my life so much! She had told us about four specific traps that Satan uses to trick us into building our self-image around. She called them the "Who am I traps."

I'd like to take some time to discuss each trap that Mrs. Landis explained to us separately and tell you how it has affected my life. Finally, I've added a fifth trap that I feel has affected me and how I view my self-image. I hope that you can relate to some of my stories and that God speaks to you through each one. There's a place for you to write your thoughts, prayers, and confessions to God dealing with each trap. After I discuss each trap, I want to reveal to you, and God wants to reveal to you, in the next chapter, how He sees us, and how He wants us to see ourselves. I hope that discovering the way God sees you and how He wants you to see yourself will free you from the bond of Satan.

THE TRAP OF PERFORMANCE
The trap that triggers us into perfectionism

From Kindergarten to eighth grade, school had always been pretty easy for me. I attended a small private school so there wasn't much competition to begin with. My graduating eighth grade class had only twenty-eight people in it. I almost always got all "A's" on every report card and I was seen as one of the "smart people." I liked being smart and I worked hard on projects and papers to make them the best they could be. For the most part I was almost always the teacher's pet, which I often jokingly got teased about when I got into Junior High. It didn't bother me much—it actually came in pretty helpful one day when I got my math teacher to give us less homework after complaining that I had a ton to do that night. (Okay, so maybe I took advantage of it from time to time.)

After I graduated from eighth grade, I began a four-year journey of – watch out! – public school. Everything about it was new to me—the teachers, the students, the rules, and just the atmosphere as a whole. And to top it all off, it was *high school*, full of so many new things to me. There were class ranks, honors classes, and competitive sports teams that literally started practicing and conditioning several months before the actual season even began. I was used to sports just being mostly about fun. If we won – awesome; if not – who cares? I soon learned that it didn't go that way in high school. The main goal was to win. Fun came on the side.

As soon as they could sit us all down at once, the guidance counselors let us have it. We were in high school now and we really had to sit up straight and pay attention; college was a mere four years away! Every grade counted, everything we did in the next four years would determine our future, we were told. You get one chance in high school and you either make it or break it.

Wow. That was a lot for us little freshman. Yet, as soon as I entered high school, being the high achiever that I was, I was immediately *determined* to come out at the top. I wanted to get an honors diploma, join the National Honors Society, be the valedictorian, etc. *This is a fresh start!* I thought. *I really want to do this right!*

And so I worked hard, took two honors classes, stressed over project after project, and toiled over getting an "A" in every class. As a freshman I was new and shy so I didn't join any clubs right off. *Next year I'll be more involved*, I thought. My freshman year ended and I had come out with "A's" in every class.

When I entered my sophomore year I was determined to do as well in my classes as I had done the year before. I remained in my two honors classes, math and English, and only allowed myself a study hall for one half of the year. After all, I wanted as many credits as I could get! Besides having so much to do with classes alone, I joined student council, French club, and ecology club. I also started off playing softball (I ended up quitting before the actual season began), which we began conditioning for in late October. Besides that, I was involved with a youth group and a dance team outside of school. Soon I began to define myself by all of the activities I was involved in. I felt that if I didn't stay so involved and perform the best of the best, I would be worthless and too "average." I wanted to be way above average, I wanted to be that stereotype we like to call "Miss High School" that was involved in anything and everything. I even hated "B's." They weren't good enough. I wanted to be the perfect high school student.

Besides, once I entered high school we were very much encouraged to do as much as we could, be involved in as many things as we could. And on top of that, we were supposed to work our butts off to get the grades to get into a good college. Class rank wasn't only something I looked at but I was told that it was something that colleges looked at. Colleges also looked at how much I was involved, I was told. *I've got to be the best!* I kept telling myself.

At the end of my sophomore year I had quit softball after playing for eight years (it's a long story!) but I was still involved with many things, inside and outside of school. Then May came around and it was time for class officer elections. I hadn't really considered running until a friend of mine convinced me to. *It would be another thing to add to my list of accomplishments and involvements. Hmm, I think I will run.* At the same time I signed up to run for class treasurer, God was speaking to me. *Don't push yourself so hard, Tessa. One of these days, you're going to burn out.* I felt as though I shouldn't run. I ran anyways. And I won. Not only did I now have that under my belt, but I also applied to be a freshman student mentor the following year. I was in the deep end, yet in my mind I wanted to be there. In my mind I was a better person because I was involved in so many ways.

Before I went back to school for my junior year I made a list of my involvements for the upcoming year so that I could actually visualize my "worth" as a student. I wanted to have a "plan of accomplishments." In the next few weeks before school started, God did a huge work in my heart and spoke to me in so many ways. *Tessa! If you want to give Me your whole, entire heart, you have to give Me more of your time, more of your life, all of your life!*

But God, that means I would have to cut back on things! All of my involvements…they're who I am! I've got two years of high school left; I've got to do everything! God still worked in my heart and told me over and over to come and be His daughter, to give everything up to know Him. I did finally regret running for class treasurer. *I should have gone with my instinct…it was God speaking to me*, I thought. Unfortunately, I only listened half-heartedly to God's convictions. I put more responsibility on myself by *starting* a club at school! I hate to think about what God was thinking when I did that. *Tessa! Don't you remember what I spoke to you? Don't you remember the work that I did in your heart?* God was still speaking to me, yet Satan's trap was still strangling me. I was stuck in the "who am I trap" of performance and Satan was loving every minute of it.

On the handout that Mrs. Landis gave to my youth group, this is how she described someone who is stuck in the "who am I trap" of performance:

Call me the perfectionist. My value and sense of worth comes from what I do and how well I do it. Whether it's athletics or academics, when I fail I often feel like I am a failure.

It described me perfectly, and I think that it describes thousands more of my peers. We've been pressured over and over to be the best that we can by the world. We're constantly getting the message that we have to stay busy and involved. *It's good for you*, they tell us. And so we begin to put our security and self-worth in how well we achieve, how well we live up to those standards. And those standards are hard! They burn us out, put loads of pressure on us, and, like the description, cause us to feel like failures if we don't live up to them. Yet those standards are so full of lies!

Have you been listening to the "who am I trap" of performance? Has it gotten a hold of you and beaten you down? Have you based your self-image and worth on how much you've achieved in life? Take some time to write your thoughts down about the trap of performance…

― ― ―

My Own Thoughts

_____

_____

_____

_____

_____

_____

_____

― ― ―

CONFESSIONS OF A GIRL

THE TRAP OF POPULARITY
It's all about a social scale

In every movie and TV having to do with kids in high school, we always hear about the same high school stereotypes that the creators are trying to portray. We hear names such as the preppies, the jocks, the nerds, the band geeks, the cheerleaders, the burnouts, and so on. And then there's always that group of rich kids living in mansions deemed the popular crowd. Okay, so I know that movies and TV shows tend to stretch reality a lot. And I know people don't go around my school making up stupid "categories," selecting different students to go in each one. Maybe they do at your school, I don't know. But I do know that whether or not we say it out loud or not, there are certain labels that we put on everyone. And when it comes down to it, you get one label or the other: popular or unpopular.

When I entered high school, there was no doubt that I wanted to be as popular as I could. I wanted to have friends, I wanted to be invited to parties, and I wanted everyone in the hallway to say "Hi" to me. My freshman year I started off by just being nice to everyone. I've always been really shy so I stuck close to my friends that had come with me from my private school. By the end of the year I had met a lot of people. I was invited to a few parties here and there and I guess you could say my popularity was "growing." I even had a boyfriend by the end of the year and we had a group of friends that we'd constantly hang out with. Life was good.

Over the summer I went to parties, hung out with my new group of friends, and I continued to get on people's "good side," I guess you could call it. At the beginning of my sophomore year I still had my boyfriend, I had a great group of friends, and people liked me. The first two months of school were very busy. There was a big birthday party almost every weekend (we were all turning the big sixteen!), including mine. I had a huge party at my house and I invited everyone I was even remotely friends with. This is going to sound horrible but I even remember thinking to myself, *When my friends from my old school come they're going to see how popular I am! I bet they'll be impressed.* When homecoming time came around I was voted to be the sophomore attendant on the homecoming court. *Wow! I really am popular,* I thought to myself. *I really am somebody at this high school.* Satan was probably cracking up at me. I was putting a huge amount of my security and worth into my popularity, and it was exactly what Satan was hoping for.

Nonetheless, my popularity dwindled down some, my boyfriend broke up with me, and I became a mess. Sure, people still liked me and I still had friends, but it wasn't like before. Remember when I was talking about running for class treasurer? It wasn't only to add an accomplishment to my involvement list. I think I partly ran just to test my popularity. I wanted to see if I still "had it in me." Did people still like me? Am I still someone? That was very shallow of me and I can't believe how much worth I was putting into my popularity.

I didn't get invited to many parties by people from school that next summer but I did make some friends in other groups. And I didn't stop basing my self-worth on how many friends I had. If people liked me and I was popular in certain crowds, good enough. I was at the point where I just wanted someone to see that I had friends. I wanted to make it known that I was still out having fun with all kinds of different people. I invited people over, held as many conversations as I could online, etc. *You've got friends, Tessa! Keep it up!*

Very few of the friends I made during the summer went to my school, and most of those friendships dwindled down to where we didn't see each other much. I had made as many friends as I could, only to find myself with hardly any real friendships.

I went on that year to make an awesome group of friends, who were all seniors. God really began to speak to me then about basing my self-worth on my popularity and who my friends were. When I first became friends with them, I said, *Tessa, a whole group of seniors! That's pretty good.* Not to mention, one of the girls in the group was the homecoming queen that fall. *Wow! I'm actually hanging out with the homecoming queen on the weekends, with a bunch of seniors!* I thought I had it all figured out.

But no. God continued to speak to me. *Tessa, people will eventually let you down. One day people will not care who was on homecoming court, how many parties you were invited to, and who you hung out with. My child, there is so much more to who you are than your popularity!*

I think that my story is much like the one that so many young people in my generation go through all the time. We fight to be known and we tell ourselves that we *have* to climb the social scale in order to be somebody. We want to be liked. We want people to be jealous of us. We want to impress people with our social standings. It's the second of Satan's "who am I traps" and it's deceiving my generation.

Has the trap of popularity gotten a hold of you? Do you define yourself by who you hang out with? Do you strive to make yourself known? Do you long to hang out with a certain group of kids deemed "cool" or "popular?" Mrs. Landis described a person caught in the popularity trap like this:

I constantly strive for the acceptance of others, and I really struggle with feelings of inadequacy when I don't get the approval of the "in crowd." It makes my day when certain people take notice of me. I need to be in that "certain circle."

Does this person describe you? It described me for too long. It really did make my day when someone "popular" took notice of me and said "Hi" to me in the hallway. Take a moment to reflect on the trap of popularity. How has it affected the way you live? How has it affected your priorities? Had you ever thought of it as a lie from Satan before?

My Own Thoughts

_____

_____

_____

_____

_____

_____

_____

THE TRAP OF POSSESSIONS
"What you have is what you are"…or so Satan tell us

I've already talked a lot about material possessions in Chapter Four but I want to look at it from a different angle. Mrs. Landis's third "who am I trap" was a trap of possessions. This is how she described someone who had been caught in that trap:

I am what I wear, or what I own. I can't imagine my life without my "stuff" or my clothes. Sometimes I find myself looking up to those who dress oh so perfectly, live in the hugest of homes or own the fastest cars.

Have you ever thought of material possessions as a way to define yourself? I have done this a lot in the past. I've simply felt better about myself just because I was wearing a certain brand or because I had a bunch of new clothes.

Over the past few years I've really struggled with the trap of possessions. I've clung to brand names and have sought after having a bunch of "stuff." I hate admitting this, but there have been times when I've felt like my life was out of control and that I had a bunch of problems but then inside I've thought to myself, *Phew! I'm going shopping tomorrow. I'll be better after that.* Many times I've looked with jealous eyes at someone else's possessions and then have tried to reassure myself, *Tessa, you have such and such…you're still better than them.* How I hate to think about those past thoughts. They really bring out an ugly side in me that I'm not proud of at all.

I think often times we not only define *our* self-image by our possessions, but we also define *others* by their possessions. Have you ever been extra nice to someone just because you knew they had more "stuff" or because they wore extra trendy clothes? I have. Have you ever looked down on someone or not wanted to reach out to someone just because you knew they weren't very wealthy? I've done it. Have you ever thought yourself better than someone else just because you knew you had more in general? Sadly, I've done that too.

We've already covered the fact that we have to choose our master: money or God. If we choose money, we'll probably end up making it the master of not only our lives and priorities but also of our thoughts about ourselves and others. If we make God our master, *He* will be the one to define who we are instead of some silly, yet serious trap set by the devil.

Have you ever met someone whom you can just tell instantly judges you by your possessions, what your wearing, the car you drive, etc.? You might not think it at first but such persons are probably throwing the exact same criticism at themselves and judging their own self-worth by the same standards. I think that there is so much insecurity among young girls out there today and I really believe that a lot of it centers round the trap of possessions. I don't know about you but after I get done looking at a fashion magazine I often get a harmful motivation to try and improve myself by buying a certain thing of a certain brand. We're bombarded with headlines that say, "You gotta have it!" We see thousands of ads showing people that seem really happy just because they're wearing a certain brand.

Do you find yourself defining yourself and others by possessions? Is your security in the clothes that you buy at the mall? Do you feel better about yourself after getting a certain thing? Take some time to write your thoughts about how Satan's trap of possessions has affected you.

— — —

My Own Thoughts

_____

_____

_____

_____

— — —

THE TRAP OF PHYSICAL APPEARANCE
Mirror, mirror on the wall

This is the trap that got me when I was young. This is the trap that's been a part of my life for quite some time. This is the trap that Satan has absolutely strangled me with. My physical appearance. My hair. The shape of my face. My nails. My teeth. *My weight.* I don't know for sure exactly when Satan began to tell me lies about my physical appearance, but I know it started a long time ago, maybe even before the donut Saturdays with my dad. The "who am I trap" of physical appearance has actually been a huge part of my life. It's been one of my biggest, longest, and hardest battles in defining my self-image and worth. Even though Satan got a hold of me at a much younger age, I'm going to start with eighth grade.

I had always been a somewhat chubby kid growing up, which my friends and I love to laugh at now. Every time we went into the little room to get weighed at school I'd always be embarrassed that I weighed more than most of my friends. I did lose some of my baby fat as I got older, but not all of it. By the time I got to eighth grade I decided that I had had enough with my "flabby" body. I went on an extreme diet. My mom practically had to force me to eat. I began to lose weight and people noticed. You probably could have called it a mild case of anorexia. It felt good. I was in control. And so a four-year-long battle with weight began.

When I entered my freshman year I saw tons of girls that were skinnier than me. I wanted so bad to be one of those girls you go up to say, "Oh my goodness, you just have the perfect body!" I wanted so badly to fit into smaller size jeans. I wanted so badly for my stomach to be completely flat. I tried as hard as I could to control my weight. The struggle continued on into my sophomore year where it became really bad. I went back and forth, trying to start over with a fresh diet almost every day. I'd wake up in the morning and say, *Okay. Today is day one of a diet. I'm going to lose weight. Today is a fresh start.* I'd go for maybe a few days eating healthily (or just not eating much) and then I'd slip and stuff food in my face, only to wind up feeling guilty, gross, and fat.

Food was constantly on my mind—how much I'd eat, when I'd eat, what I'd eat, how many calories I'd eaten that day, etc. The winter of my sophomore year I wrote the following in my journal:

My Struggle
I'm not sure anyone realizes my daily struggle to lose weight, to eat right, to look good in a bathing suit for Florida. It's not just a struggle. It's almost my life. Sometimes no one knows my obsession with my weight. I'm not fat. I'm not skinny. I struggle. Not a DAY goes by where I can eat whatever I want without thinking about how it will affect me, wondering what I can do to make up for it, or feeling guilty for shoving food when I'm not even hungry. Food has become an enemy that I over-indulge in and it is my struggle. But no one knows this struggle. Only the part of my brain that goes off with every single thing I put in my mouth. Everything. Not kidding. That's my struggle, and I hate it.

Again on March 8 I wrote:

Dear Lord,

Please give me patience and self-control (regarding food). Lord, it is time to end my struggle. Lord, do something amazing and lift this burden from my soul and heart and life. I want to be free. I don't want to think about food and my weight.

I wanted so bad to be set free, to love myself for who I was on the inside rather than what I saw on the outside. But I just kept obsessing about my weight. And as the months passed, I began to not only worry about my weight but also about every other thing on the outside. I tried to have perfect hair, perfect nails, the perfect outfits, the perfect skin etc. I'd been filling my mind with unrealistic images I saw in magazines, on TV, and in movies. Simply going through a fashion magazine would not only leave me feeling as though I needed more possessions as I mentioned earlier, but it also left me with more harmful motivation to make my physical appearance perfect. The models in there had perfect bodies, perfect skin, and perfect hair. *If they're perfect, why can't I try and make myself perfect?* I thought.

As I look at the table of contents of a popular magazine for young women, which I won't name, these are some of the names of the articles: "Look sexier in jeans," "Zap your zits (in just one day)," and "The truth about carbs." I would look at so many magazines similar to this one and I just kept on building my self-image around what I saw in the mirror. I put a lot of money into trying to buy the right products and the right clothes. Sometimes my nails would look nice, sometimes I'd have a good tan, but I was always left wanting to be more perfect on the outside. I was always left feeling as though there was something more I needed to do, another product I needed to buy.

Weight continued to be the number one struggle for me. I even went to my mom a couple of times and admitted it to her and asked her for prayer. I know God was trying to get a hold of me during those times but I just kept resisting Him and kept obsessing over the scale. I'd rejoice if the scale said I lost two pounds and then three days later I'd be feeling guilty because I'd lost control over my eating again and the scale was going to show it the next morning. My obsession was definitely causing me to drift further away from God. Over and over I'd hear people say that God loves us just the way we are, and I believed it, but I wanted to look good in the eyes of others, and most of all, myself. I constantly compared myself to other girls, eyeing their bodies up and down to see if they were skinnier or more in shape than me. My eyes became the eyes of envy as soon as I saw someone with a better body than mine. I was longing to be the picture perfect size two and God was waiting to set me free.

It's funny because if I had written about this topic earlier in the book I wouldn't have been able to say that I'd been set free yet. I would have told you that it was still a huge burden on my shoulders, a trap that I was still caught in every second of my life. Hopefully I would have simply told you that I was working on it, and would have encouraged you to do the same if you were sharing in my struggle.

God knew better than to have me write this chapter first, because last week I was set free from my struggle with weight. My youth group was on a missions trip in Columbus and we were having a serious time of worship. When it was over we were informed that the guys and the girls were going to split up for a time of prayer and confession. I don't think I had ever realized the power of confession. The girls got in a corner and as we cried and passed around the Kleenex boxes we poured out our secret sins and prayed for one another. When it came time for me to sit in the middle of the circle, it was heavy on my heart that I needed to confess my four-year-long battle with my weight. My voice shaky and my face wet with tears, I confessed it to the girls and youth leaders around me. God did something so amazing in my heart that night. He set me free of my battle with my weight. It's no longer a secret lurking inside of my heart that laughs at me when I look in the mirror. Satan has been defeated and I've escaped his "who am I trap" of physical appearance. I can't promise that I'll never struggle with my weight again because I know that some days I'm going to stumble and fall. Some days my human nature is going to get the better of me and I'm going to put myself back in the trap. But I can rest assured now, that even if I fall for a day, God is so ready and willing to pick me right back up the next day and remind me of the freedom He granted me. I am *not* only the reflection in the mirror. And neither are you.

Have you been struggling with the trap of physical appearance? Mrs. Landis described someone struggling with this trap like this:

> *Perfection in the outward appearance is a big priority. I'd sacrifice anything for that perfect bod that seems to be out there somewhere. I often end up comparing myself to others in this realm, always hoping to come out on top.*

Do my struggles relate to your own? Maybe instead of weight you've been obsessing over something else dealing with your outward appearance. Take some time to write down your thoughts and prayers about the trap of physical appearance.

— — —

My Own Thoughts

_____

_____

THE TRAP OF AFFIRMATION
What did you say about me?

I made up the last "who am I" trap myself and I call it the trap of affirmation—basing your self-worth on what others (besides God) say and think of you. When you base your self-worth and define who you are under the trap of affirmation you wait for praise or compliments from others in order to feel good about yourself.

I've struggled a lot with the trap of affirmation. Many times I've measured my self-image according to what guys have said about me. If a guy flirted with me or said something to compliment me, it was a like a foundation that I could fall back on if I needed to. Sometimes I would even direct my conversations with guys in order for them to say something good about me. It was as though I was hungering for someone of the opposite sex to just show me they approved of me and thought I was extra special.

I think that a lot of girls my age struggle with the trap of affirmation whether it is from guys or girls. We just want someone to tell us that we're "beautiful" or "sexy" or "soooo cute" all the time.

In these days we put so much value into what others say about us, as though others' opinions are always the truth. I had to learn the hard way that if I go around trying to get guys to affirm me as a person to feel as though I was somebody unique and loved, I was going to be let down from time to time, which would leave me feeling like a nobody.

How can you tell if you're stuck in the trap of affirmation? Try asking yourself these questions:

- If I'm feeling bad about myself do I purposely go and talk to a guy that I know will give me a compliment or affirmation?

- When my self-image turns crummy is it because I'm thinking about what someone else has said about me?

- When I'm talking to people, especially guys, do I purposely fish for compliments to feel better about myself?

There's nothing wrong with someone paying us a compliment, but if we're holding on to compliments and affirmation from others for dear life to boost our own self-image, we're stuck in Satan's trap of affirmation. Has Satan gotten you into this trap?

— — —

My Own Thoughts

_____

_____

_____

_____

WHO'S THAT IN THE MIRROR? THE FALSE IMAGE WE'VE FORMED

Chapter 6

Looking Through The Father's Eyes: The Truth To Who We Are

1 Samuel 16:7, "...The Lord does not look at the things man looks at. Man looks at the outward appearance, but the Lord looks at the heart." (NIV)

Terry Pluto, a writer for my local newspaper wrote an article once that really encouraged me. Not only is he a sports columnist, but he also writes for the "Everyday Faith" page. I thought his point of view was really interesting. The article was entitled "Women's value isn't in looks." Here's part of it:

I was in a hospital waiting room the other day, and the TV was stuck on a daytime talk show aimed at women. The subject was ladies need a certain bathing suit – starting at $80 – to make their figures more pleasing to the eye. "Sure, there's some padding," oozed one of the guests. "But it sure beats plastic surgery, doesn't *it?" Then came a commercial demanding the women work out like marathon runners to get in shape—now! I don't know the name of the show and I don't care. I was just astounded by the verbal assaults on women. There was a commercial that basically said, "Hey lady, you stink! You need this kind of deodorant." Of course, you also need this special mouthwash, because your breath is enough to topple the Terminal Tower. Drop weight, but get a bigger chest. Buy clothes you really don't want because you don't want to look like a blob, do you? And your hair...darling... you've got to do something with that! Looks like you've got a family of eagles living there. There also were commercials about how to handle headaches, heartburn, and stomach problems. Dare I mention Preparation H or some female unmentionables that are constantly mentioned on daytime TV? Watch this stuff for a while and it's amazing every woman doesn't feel totally overwhelmed, utterly inferior and on the verge of neurosis. Why? Because TV tells women: No one will ever love you unless you color your hair, throw out your clothes and eat nothing but seaweed until 2009.*

Why write about this on the faith page? Because women are under attack—and it seems most of it is coming from other women. Far more than young men, women are telling you that you're too fat or too thin. Too short or too tall. You look too young or too old. The Bible says in Psalm 139 that each of us is "fearfully and wonderfully made." But a commercial screams back, "Not in those shoes." Ladies, here's a secret: Guys aren't looking at your shoes unless you happen to be in heels so high you keep falling over.

Guys don't care about women's shoes. Guys don't talk about women's shoes. Or purses. Want to waste some time? Ask a guy, "What do you think of my purse?" At best, you'll get a grunt or a yawn. Ladies, give it a rest. Tell the fashion police and plastic surgeons and everyone else who wants to destroy your self-esteem, well, tell them to shove it. Use Proverbs 31:30: "Charm is deceptive, beauty is fleeting, but a woman who loves and fears the Lord is to be praised." When will we ever hear a commercial for that?

God made us special. Why else would every *person have different fingerprints, voiceprints and DNA? In the end, people will either accept us—or they won't. Who does your nails has absolutely nothing to do with it...*

> © *Copyright. Akron Beacon Journal. All Rights Reserved. Distributed by Knight Ridder Digital.*

Satan has caused the young women in this generation to look down on themselves. How badly I wish that we could only begin to see ourselves through the eyes of our Heavenly Father. His image of us is so completely different from that of the world and our own. The verse quoted at the beginning of the chapter says it all: "… *but the Lord looks at the heart.*"

When I read this verse or drift off into thoughts about how God looks at His children I have to ask myself: does God even notice our physical features? Does He even use words like fat, skinny, and ugly? When God looks at us does He say things like, "There she goes, gaining weight again" or "I wish she'd do something different with her hair, she could really use an update" or "She really needs to start hanging out with the 'in crowd' more often?" I really don't think so. It makes me laugh just to think about God saying something like that. He simply doesn't look at people the same way the world does, and if we could only realize that, we'd be living in so much more freedom! And if we could only realize that His picture of us is the only one that truly matters in this life, so many chains would be cast off, so many hearts redeemed from Satan's grasp.

I think that so many times my problem is remembering the fact that I'm living life for an ultimate audience of One—the One who gave me eternal life with Him. Sometimes I think to myself, *Well, I already know what God thinks of me. He loves me a whole lot, thinks I'm great, etc. But I want the world to think these things of me! I want to look in the mirror and think that about myself! I want the world to love me, and to think I'm a wonderful person! The opinion of God is great, but, I've got other impressions to make here and now.* I suddenly forget who I'm living for. I forget the ultimate purpose of my life here on earth: not to please others, not to please myself, but to please God, to live with a passion for His plan for my life, to fall in love with Him, and to follow His words. Instead of listening to God's opinions I listen to the ones around me—from magazines, from movies, from peers, from TV shows, and from myself.

So how does God really see us? Thankfully, when my old teacher, Mrs. Landis, came to talk to us, she didn't leave us hanging after explaining to us Satan's deadly "who am I traps." She showed us a bunch of different verses in the Bible that talked about how God really sees us, and who we really are. Maybe you'll have never heard these truths before or maybe you've heard them over and over but you can't quite come to the point where you actually believe God is talking about you. Whatever the case, believe them today, because they are not demanding traps, but pure truth—they are the very word of God. So, here's how Mrs. Landis laid it out for us…this is "who we are really."

You Were Created in God's Image
Genesis 1:26-28 "Then God said, 'Let us make man in our image, in our likeness, and let them rule over the fish of the sea and the birds of the air, over the livestock, over all the earth, and over all the creatures that move along the ground.' So God created man in his own image, in the image of God he created him; male and female he created them." (NIV)

Created in God's image. It's so incredibly easy to overlook this verse when we're reading about creation in Genesis. A lot of us have probably heard or read the story a bunch of times. We read about when God created the animals, the fish, day and night, the land, the moon and the stars, and so on, and then when we get to His creation of man, we casually read over it and pay no special attention to a totally amazing thing! *We were created in the image of God? Whoa. The God of the Universe created mere human beings, knowing they'd be sinners, to bear a resemblance to His extravagant radiance?* It's really a huge thing. It's like when we resemble one of our parents or a sibling. When two parents have a child, the child will share in their genes and as a result have some of the same unique features in hair color, eye color, nose shape, etc.

Do you really and truly believe that when God created you He made you to resemble His very nature *and character*? Believe it! God created every single person with a piece of Him inside! It's like having God's genes passed down to us, but they're not just any genes. They're genes of righteousness, holiness, love, pure beauty, and every other characteristic of God – and they're in us! It's pretty wow to me!

The other awesome thing is that even though we were all created from the same source—God—He created us all totally unique, *no* two people alike.

I absolutely just love to sit and people watch, especially in the middle of a busy place like the mall. It's so interesting to me to just see *so* many different personalities and reactions and facial gestures and body language and different styles and so on. There are so many people out there and it just baffles my mind that *no* two people are exactly the same! Sometimes I just sit and think, *what a creative God*! I can't believe that there are roughly six billion people in the world and since Adam, the first man, was created, there haven't been any duplicates.

Sure, sometimes there are people that look so much alike it's scary. And of course there are identical twins and such, but there's never two individuals with the exact same physical appearance, talents, personality, etc. God purposely made you unique and He's absolutely crazy about you!

I once heard someone tell me that God actually dreamed up my personality. I had never thought about that before. God didn't just quick throw me together with a pinch of this and a pinch of that, but He actually took the time to carefully create every single feature about me and my persona as a whole. He purposely made me to love ice cream and chocolate and dancing. He purposely created me as an introvert, shy and quiet spoken. Psalms 139:15 says, "You know me inside and out, you know every bone in my body. You know exactly how I was made, bit by bit, how I was sculpted from nothing into something." (Msg)

From nothing into something. To God, you *are* something, a very precious and unique something—His very own creation that He's wild for! And not only are you unique, but you're in God's very own image. How our generation has missed this truth! How we long for one particular body type, a particular achievement, a particular gain. But God says, "Look, my child! You are made in the image of the Creator of the Universe who's perfect in every way—perfect in righteousness and love and so much more! What more could you ask for?"

There isn't more we could ask for, and if only we could realize that. If only we could realize that our uniqueness, inside and out, was given to us on purpose, and as much as we love it or hate it, God loves it and is so full of the pride of a parent when He looks at you.

Never let this thought leave your heart: *You were created in God's image, unique and beautiful! There is not one single person like you and your precious Heavenly Father would have it no other way! He formed you with delicate creativity and precision.*

My Own Thoughts
Do you truly believe that you are totally unique and that God created you that way on purpose? List 3 unique things about you:

_____

_____

_____

_____

_____

_____

_____

How does it make you feel to know that God created you in His very own image? Have you accepted that as a truth in your life? How does it change the way you view yourself?

You Were Redeemed at a Great Price
1 Corinthians 6:20, "You were bought at a price…" (NIV)

Before you read this section, read John 19 in your Bible. What exactly does it mean to redeem something? I looked up the word "redeem" in the thesaurus and some words and phrases that came up were "trade in," "exchange" and "buy back." I love the last one the most and I think it perfectly describes God's redemption for us. *We were bought back into eternal life with Christ at a huge price.* What price did God pay for us? His only son.

Okay, I want you to really, really think about this, because I know for many of us it's something we've heard over and over and over. Some of you can probably even quote John 3:16 right off the bat with your eyes closed while turning around in circles:

"For God so loved the world that he gave his one and only Son, that whoever believes in Him shall not perish but have eternal life." (NIV)

Seriously, I heard this verse so many times growing up that it almost came to mean nothing to me. God loved the world. He gave His only Son, Jesus, to die on the cross for me so I could go to heaven. I heard the story in Sunday school and saw the characters on the boards acting out the story. I heard the story read during the Easter season. I heard it several times growing up in my Christian school. It had become a mere fact to me, instead of something I truly took to heart when I tried to answer the question, "who am I?"

So how else does God see us besides unique and created in His own image? He sees us with a huge amount of worth—so much worth that He risked sending His only Son to Earth to enter into the human realm and suffer as a human suffers, and to die as a human dies.

The other day my dad and I were talking about God's unconditional love, how He just keeps on loving and loving, even after we mess up over and over and over. As humans, when we're helping someone out and trying to love them as much as we can, we want to get the same treatment back. We want results. If we're trying to help turn someone's life around, we want to see changes. We want to know that we're going to get good results back from our time, effort, and generosity. Maybe we give money to others to try to help them get back on track. Maybe we give our time (which is just as costly!) to talk to someone for hours, trying to help and encourage that person, or even just trying to build a solid friendship. Often times, when we don't see changes, or when we don't get the same love back or the same effort put into the relationship from the other person, we tend to get frustrated and easily give up trying to love that person. We think, *They've messed up for the last time! They're finished in my book. They're not worth it!*

Thank goodness that God's not human. If God looked down on earth those thousands of years ago and said, "I'm going to send my Son to die, but only if people are going to be perfect after that!" Well, it wouldn't have happened! God knew that even after He sent His only Son to die for the sins of the world that people would still continue to mess up and break His heart day after day. But He took that risk simply because He loved us with an amazing and unconditional love. God had the perfect Son, and He gave up that Son to save an imperfect world, a world that He knew wouldn't even return the same love back to Him.

Do you realize how much God sacrificed just so that He could spend eternity with *you*? Before this year, I always had this thought in my mind, even after I heard the phrase "He died for YOU" over and over, saying *how am I anyone special if Christ died for the entire world? How do I know He wasn't just thinking, "Well, I really want to die for and save so and so, so I guess while I'm at it I'll just include Tessa."* That thought caused me to underestimate the power of Jesus' love and salvation and what He did for me.

I had just returned home from seeing the big movie of the year, *The Passion of the Christ* by Mel Gibson. My church had rented out an entire theatre and I had gone with a group of my friends. To say the least, the movie was very powerful. I gained a great sense of what Jesus really went through when He died on the cross. I left with a new picture in my mind of *what* Christ went through when He died for our sins. However, I don't think I left the movie with a new sense of *who* Christ did it for. I still had the thought in my mind: *I've heard it over and over that Christ's love for me was shown when He died on the cross for my sins; but how can I say that it was for me as an individual? How do I really know that God was thinking of me when He went through all that?*

Well, I went home from the movie and my parents and sisters and I started discussing it. I told my mom how it's so easy for me to think what I did, and she told me something that I had never heard before, and it completely changed my view. She told me, "You have to remember, Tessa, that even if you were the only person on earth, Jesus still would have gone through what He did, just so that you could join Him in heaven one day."

Whoa. That definitely made me think. After seeing such a gruesome, bloody, and graphic, yet *realistic*, picture of the terrorizing and gut-wrenching pain that Jesus went through, I could hardly believe it. *I'm worth* that *much to God? He wants me to be in paradise with Him one day* that *much*? The answer is yes, yes, yes! It is true. If there was no one else living on earth besides you, Jesus still would have gone through his awful death on the cross so that you would be by His side one day. Doesn't knowing that fact simply make you feel worth more than diamonds? It should, because you are. And God thinks you are.

― ― ―

My Own Thoughts
Have you ever taken the time to realize the price at which you were bought back to eternal life with God? How does it change the way you think about yourself to know that Christ would have suffered through the same death even if you were the only person to gain anything from it?

_____

_____

_____

_____

_____

_____

_____

― ― ―

CONFESSIONS OF A GIRL

You Were Adopted into Royalty

Romans 8:14-17, "Because those who are led by the Spirit of God are sons of God. For you did not receive a spirit that makes you a slave again to fear, but you received the Spirit of sonship. And by him we cry, 'Abba, Father.' The Spirit himself testifies with our spirit that we are God's children. Now if we are children, then we are heirs – heirs of God and co-heirs with Christ, if indeed we share in his sufferings in order that we may also share in his glory." (NIV)

What is it about royalty that captures our hearts? How many of us can say that when we were young we didn't at least once dream of being a beautiful princess living in a huge palace, dancing around in a tiara with our Prince Charming? There's just something about the exquisite ball gowns, the lavish life and the graceful elegance of a fairytale-like princess—it all sounds so appealing to our feminine hearts.

When I was in 8th grade, a bunch of the girls in my class went to a weekend conference called "In Search of a Princess." It was in a huge Hilton Hotel in Columbus where we were treated to beautiful and top-notch rooms, unlike any hotel I had seen or stayed in before! The purpose of the weekend was to make us feel special and valued and show a clear picture of who we were in Christ–His daughters in His royal family whom He was absolutely crazy about! We were pampered with fun things like little spa samples so we could do face masks and such, and we were even given the chance to dress up and have a fun photo taken with our friends for a memento. It was so much fun that weekend for us girls to get just a little taste of royalty–something we didn't normally get to experience in our everyday lives.

But the main thing we learned that weekend was that we are, in fact royalty! It doesn't just have to be a worldly dream, a wish, or a fantasy. It can be a reality, and for those of us who have already made Jesus the Lord of our lives it already is a reality – we *are* royalty – in its highest form in the universe. And it's a royalty that can never be taken away from us. No one can ever denounce our position in the royal family, or overthrow the King and His royal family, His daughters included.

The verses quoted earlier in Romans 8 give us this promise. When we ask God into our hearts and lives, we receive the Holy Spirit, but not just any spirit, we're told, but a spirit of *sonship*! We become God's very own children and because we are His children, we are also heirs of God. And then it goes on to say something that really sticks out to me the most in this verse–we are *co-heirs* with Christ himself! We actually get to share His inheritance among ourselves, because He is God's Son, and we become God's daughters – a part of the same family!

Ephesians 1:5 says, "He predestined us to be adopted as his sons through Jesus Christ, in accordance with His pleasure and will." Now, read this verse in a different way and fill in your name in the blank:

"He predestined _____ to be adopted as his daughter through Jesus Christ, in accordance with His pleasure and will"

Before you were even created, conceived, and born into the world, God predetermined that you would be adopted into His family one day as His royal daughter, worthy of sharing an inheritance with Christ himself. And it was not only God's *will* to do this, but it was His *pleasure*! That part of the verse really sticks out to me. When God adopted us into His royal family it wasn't just something He knew He needed to do, but it was something that He took joy in doing! He is *so* in love with you, His creation, that He wanted you to be able to take part in His royalty.

What an amazing truth to live by: That we are God's royalty, we are His daughters, and He takes amazing joy in taking us into His family. When you question who you are, remember that if you have accepted Christ into your life you are royalty. You couldn't ask for a higher position or a more valuable inheritance.

My Own Thoughts
Have you ever dreamed of being royalty? How does it change your view of yourself to know that royalty is something you're adopted into when you make Jesus the Lord of your life?

LOOKING THROUGH THE FATHER'S EYES: THE TRUTH TO WHO WE ARE

You are Treasured by God

Zephaniah 3:17, "The Lord your God is with you, He is mighty to save. He will take great delight in you, He will quiet you with His love, He will rejoice over you with singing." (NIV)

We were created in God's image. We are unique. We were bought back into eternal life at a huge price. We were adopted into royalty. *And we are treasured by the King of Kings.* The King of Kings, the God above all gods, the Ruler of the Universe, takes *great delight in you*!

If you grew up in a Christian home like me, you may have heard Psalms 139 quoted over and over to you, like John 3:16. But I think it's another one of those passages of scripture that we almost become immune to and we begin to underestimate its power and truth. Maybe you've never heard Psalms 139. Whether you know it by heart or this is your first time reading it, read it now and really taste its truth:

Psalms 139:13-16, "For you created my inmost being; you knit me together in my mother's womb. I praise you because I am fearfully and wonderfully made; your works are wonderful, I know that full well. My frame was not hidden from you when I was made in the secret place. When I was woven together in the depths of the earth, your eyes saw my unformed body. All the days ordained for me were written in your book before one of them came to be." (NIV)

Now read it in another version:

"Oh yes, you shaped me first inside, then out; you formed me in my mother's womb. I thank you, High God—you're breathtaking! Body and soul, I am marvelously made! I worship in adoration—what a creation! You know me inside and out, you know every bone in my body; you know exactly how I was made, bit by bit, how I was sculpted from nothing into something. Like an open book, you watched me grow from conception to birth; all the stages of my life were spread out before you, the days of my life all prepared before I'd even lived one day." (Msg)

You are not an accident. It doesn't matter whether your parents meant to have you or not. It doesn't matter if you weren't part of the "plan." You were part of the Creator's plan. God *knew*, even before you were conceived, how you would live *every single day* of your life. He shaped every single bit of you with the highest amount of care. God *never* messes up when He creates someone. His works are *wonderful*, and that includes you. People are God's greatest creation, His most marvelous work! And when God looks at you, He sees someone so beautiful. In Psalms 45:11 the Bible says, "The King is enthralled by your beauty." Enthralled. Fascinated. Captivated. Awestruck. Those are words that describe how God sees you. He is so amazed at the awesomeness of His creation. He *treasures* us. And as Zephaniah 2:17 says, He takes great delight in us!

Perhaps you have a poor self-image because Satan has tried to convince you that you're worthless. Maybe you feel as if you don't mean anything to anybody, but you're only a waste of space. Perhaps you were adopted and you feel unwanted by your birth mother and father. Maybe your mother or father turned to drugs or alcohol instead of taking care of you and in turn you feel abandoned. Finally, maybe you've been physically, verbally, or sexually abused one time or several times over and it left you feeling dirty, unloved, guilty, and useless. Whatever your story is, hear this promise: You are precious and cherished by your Heavenly Father and you always will be. Nothing on Earth can take away His feelings for you, nothing that you do or anyone else does. His love for you is eternal. Bind this truth to your heart, and let it forever change the way you feel about yourself.

My Own Thoughts
Has someone or something left you feeling like an ugly speck of dirt? How does it feel to know that, in reality, you are eternally treasured by the Creator and Ruler of all things?

_____

_____

_____

_____

_____

_____

_____

A NEW PERSPECTIVE
I hope you have found one

On Mrs. Landis's handout that she left us with was this:

Your choice: Do you listen to what the world says about you or what God says about you?
The result: Bondage to the traps or freedom to be who God intended you to be.

We have to make that choice. We have to choose who we're going to listen to. We have to choose whose opinion we're going to live for—God's or the world's. We have to choose bondage in Satan's traps or freedom in who God has told us we really are—unique, bought back, royalty, and priceless treasures that He takes great pleasure in.

I'm going to choose freedom, and I hope that you will too. If the young women and girls of this generation can begin to gain a new identity, a new self-worth based upon God's words and standards and not the world's, many chains of self-hatred will be broken, and God's purpose for our lives will be further accomplished. The next time you look in the mirror, remember the truth. Your face will shine with all the beautiful radiance of a girl that knows who she is in Christ. Trust me, there's nothing more beautiful!

WHEN IT'S ALL SAID AND DONE
A summary on self-image

- The young women and girls living in my generation too often have a false self-image.

- Satan has used the world to tell us where to go to build a better self-image. He has set up "who am I traps" that trick us into getting our self-worth from our performance in work, school, and sports, our popularity, our possessions, our physical appearance, and the acceptance and affirmation we get from others, especially guys.

- We need to learn to look to God's word to define our self-image and worth, because, not only is it completely opposite of what the world tells us, but it is the truth.

- We may think that what God thinks about us doesn't even matter, but all that matters is what the world thinks here and now. However, when we come to that point in our thinking we have to remember Who we're ultimately living for—Jesus Christ. His opinion is all that truly matters now and for eternity.

- When we look to see what God says about us we find that we were created in His righteous image, we are unique, and we were bought back into eternal life at an enormous cost. We also find that when we accept God's salvation into our lives we become adopted into His family, and therefore we become royalty and share in Christ's inheritance. Finally, we find that we are God's greatest creation, and we are wonderfully made. God treasures and cherishes every single one of us no matter who we are, where we come from, or what we've done.

– – –

FINAL STEPS TO SEEING YOURSELF THROUGH GOD'S EYES

As young women with a mission from God to change this generation and turn it towards the truth, we must not go any further until we can come face to face with ourselves and be completely honest about our self-image. How do you see yourself? When you look in the mirror are you looking through God's eyes or the world's? Why do you think this is?

Satan will use whatever he can to give us a false image of ourselves and we must not only pinpoint the lies he's telling us but *how he's getting those lies through to us.* The obvious (and easiest) answer would be: society. But look deeper than just a broad and general place.

Is there a certain magazine that, after you've looked at it, it leaves you feeling worthless and ugly? Or maybe it leaves you feeling like a nobody because you can't afford to buy all the products and clothes and "toys" in it. That's Satan working as hard as he can and we have to fight back. Don't read the magazine. Avoid the magazine rack at the drug store. Cancel your subscription. Do whatever it takes to get Satan off your back; and remember, God is fighting for you, not against you. He will give you the strength and help that you need.

Is there a certain character on TV that makes you feel bad about yourself? Don't watch the TV show. Does hanging around certain people make you feel like a lousy underachiever? Don't hang out with them as much. We're in a battle to hold on tightly to the truth—don't let Satan deceive you; and get rid of the things in your life that He's using to manipulate you.

If you have to, start your day off by reading the verses of truth throughout this chapter. They're an awesome daily reminder, that will help you when you're tempted to fall into Satan's "who am I" traps. You could even write them down on note cards and keep them somewhere close to you during the day so you can look at them whenever you want. Think it sounds cheesy to whip out some verses in the middle of math class when you find yourself about to take a snooze? It's not, and the more you pound the words into your heart and mind, the more you're going to believe them, and the more you're going to hide them in your heart.

– – –

My Own Thoughts
What are some steps you need to take today to begin building a better self-image? Is there a certain thing or person that Satan is trying to use against you?

_____
_____
_____
_____
_____
_____
_____

- - -

I want to leave you with something that one of my camp counselors sent to me a few years ago. Think of it as God speaking about you, His daughter. Read it every day, and let the words sink into your heart.

> *I made her…she is different. She is unique. With love I formed her in her mother's womb. I fashioned her with great joy. I remember, with great pleasure, the day I created her. I love her smile. I love her ways. I love to hear her laugh and the silly things she says and does. She brings me great pleasure. This is how I made her (Psalms 139:13-17). I made her pretty and not beautiful, because I knew her heart, and I knew it would be in vain…I wanted her to search out her heart and to learn it would be Me in her that would draw her friends to her (1 Peter 3:3-5). I made her in such a way that she would need me. I made her a little more lonely than she would like to be …only because I need for her to learn and depend on Me…I know her heart, I know if I had not made her like*

this she would go her chosen way and forget Me... her Creator (Psalms 62:5-8). I have given her many good and happy things because I love her (Romans 8:32). Because I love her, I have seen her broken heart and the tears she thinks she has cried alone...I have cried with her, and had a broken heart too (Psalms 56:8). Often she has fallen and stumbled only because she would not hold My hand. So many lessons she's learned the hard way because she would not listen to my voice (Isaiah 53:5). So many times I watch her return to My arms, sad and broken (Isaiah 66:2). I have to reshape her and remold her...to renew her to what I planned her to be. It has not been easy for her or for Me (Jeremiah 29:11). And now she is mine again...I made her and I bought her back because I love her (Romans 5:8). I want her to be conformed to My image ...this high goal I have set for her because I love her (2 Corinthians 2:14).

— — —

Chapter 7

Modesty: A New Approach

1 Timothy 2:9 "I also want women to dress modestly, with decency and propriety…" (NIV)

I've shared my heart with you about relationships, materialism, and self-image—all issues that I feel strongly about, and all issues that have affected my life in a major way. Not to mention, they're all issues that are easily brought to the table. I think every girl could openly admit that she struggles from time to time with at least one of those things. But now I want to talk about something else that I've learned a lot about lately, an issue that maybe we haven't thought about enough, but an issue that very much needs to be dealt with: modesty. I can already hear you groaning. I can picture your eyes rolling back towards your head. *Modesty? What an old-fashioned word! To be modest you practically have to cover up your whole body—where's the cuteness in that? Modest people are so out of touch with fashion. It's definitely not an issue.*

If those are your thoughts, then this chapter is definitely for you, because I want to talk about modesty in a way you might not have heard before. Modesty does not mean that you can't dress in style. It doesn't mean you can never look adorable in an outfit again—if that were the case then I'd join you in the eye rolling and I probably wouldn't even want to write about modesty in the first place. It doesn't mean you have to wear long, baggy t-shirts with no flattering elements whatsoever (unless you want to go back to the eighties styles, which – brace yourself – are coming back into style). No, modesty doesn't mean any of those things and, sadly, I believe that too many girls in this generation think that modesty *does* mean those things. And when you define it in that stereotypical way, it comes off as boring, unattractive, and maybe even snobby or prudish. And no girl wants to be any of those things.

But not only have I learned a different (and real) definition of modesty, but I've also learned the importance of it and *why* God commanded women to be modest in 1 Timothy 2:9. (See beginning of chapter.) He didn't command us to be modest for no reason, and His command was not one that He meant only for women back in Bible times. He put it in the Bible for us to see, hear, and obey *today,* in this generation.

Unfortunately, we're living in a world where true modesty has gone out the window. It hardly even exists. I find that I walk into the mall and have a hard time finding a pair of shorts anymore that cover a decent portion of my legs. And no, I'm not looking for shorts that go down to my knees.

Skirts are no better. Of course, you can always find the "little past the knees" style, which is still very cute, but mini skirts just *had* to come back in style! Mini skirts with ruffles, and flowers, and layers—every kind. And I'm talking *mini*. *Barely there*. And you know what I think? The skirts could be really cute—I actually really like a lot of them. But the fact that they practically show everything just kills it. And in the end I don't even get to wear the skirts for the fact that I really don't want to expose half my underwear when I sit down.

The other day I walked into a store and just stared in amazement at one of the mini skirts that was being sold. I was thinking, *Where's the rest of this thing*??! It looked like a once-cute skirt that was cut in half! *Does no one give any care to what they're wearing anymore*? I really don't think they do. I think it's come to the point where it really doesn't even matter how much skin we're showing.

And not only are we encouraged to show our bottom half as sexily as possible, but we're bombarded with styles that show off our top halves just as much. Whether it's short shirts (short enough to show that adorable little belly button ring!), low necklines, or (literally) see through material, you'll find the style out there—whether it's flattering or not. The message we get is: *However you dress, just make sure you look attractive and sexy. Make people want you. Make heads turn.* Sexy, sexy, sexy. That's what young women want to be. What happened to words like "elegant" and "classy?" They seem to have disappeared, that's for sure.

About two years ago I remember my mom telling my sisters and me one day after church about something a lady had said to her. The lady had two sons who were in the tween-teen stage. She went up to my mom and told her how much she appreciated the modest way my sisters and I dressed. *Wow*, I thought, *I never knew it was that big a deal or that what I was wearing was actually making a difference*. I was surprised to know that someone was actually watching me and the way I presented myself. Yet, I was also somewhat surprised that she was speaking about me. Am I all that modest? Do I really dress much more modestly than other girls? Compared to some girls I knew I could answer an honest "yes," but what's the point of comparing? I needed to look at myself and no one else.

Modesty has never really been the easiest thing for me. I've been blessed enough in the long run to have a mother that kept a close eye on what my sisters and I wore, especially in public. Of course, when I was younger I wasn't wise enough to appreciate her efforts.

I remember when I was in fifth grade and spaghetti strap shirts became real popular. Everyone was wearing them. Well, my mom had a rule. We couldn't wear them unless we were wearing a tank top underneath to cover our bra straps and just for more coverage in general. I remember having stupid little arguments with my mom over it. "But Mom! So and so's allowed to wear them! It doesn't look bad!" I can't remember if I won any of those arguments but I do know that most times my mom came out the winner—a tank top underneath it was.

And as the years went on my mom continued to monitor our wardrobes. She'd look at us before we went out. Were our jeans too tight? Were our shirts too short or too low or too tight? She let us know if they were, and it brought up many stupid little arguments that could have so easily been avoided if I had been mature enough to realize why she was doing what she was doing.

The reason that modesty has many times been a hard thing for me to deal with is because I really love fashion. I love putting random things together to create unique and fun outfits. I get excited when I can go into a thrift store and buy an abandoned scarf for ninety cents and then bring it home and make an outfit out of it. I guess you could even call it a little hobby of mine to come up with outfits that, at first glance, you might say wouldn't work. It might sound kind of ridiculous, but I know there's some of you out there that can relate to me. Dressing is something *fun*. I love watching the styles change and I love to observe what other girls are wearing and appreciate all the creativity that some put into their outfits. I think that allowing fashion to be something creative and unique is such a fun part about being a girl. We get to choose from so many different styles, whereas with guys there are only a few different options. We get to spice up our outfits with jewelry and hair accessories and purses.

With such an interest and love for fashion, not only has it been hard for me to be content with what's in my closet, but it's also been hard for me to watch what I put into my closet. When I go shopping I'm instantly surrounded with styles that tempt me to show more skin than I know I should. It's tempting to talk myself into thinking a shirt is too loose (when really it fits fine) and go for the next smallest size that fits a little too tightly. And sometimes I've given in to that temptation, only to regret it later.

I know I'm not the only girl going through this. How do I know this? Because it's an obvious fact that as girls, whether we enjoy fashion or not, there's a longing inside each one of us to be attractive. We like to look nice and we want others to acknowledge that. Whether we express it or not, we secretly love it when a guy turns his head when we walk by with an approving look on his face. It's a part of our human nature to want to be told we're beautiful. It makes us feel good inside.

Modesty is something I feel so strongly about because I've learned that dressing is something that God cares a great deal about. Dressing is even something that I can do to honor and glorify God or something I can do to dishonor Him, and in the meantime, possibly cause a world of destruction among others around me.

How on earth can you cause any kind of destruction by what you wear? Dressing is not something that has anything to do with God, anyways. Why does He care what I wear? He has way more important things to care about and besides, if I were to go shopping with God, there's no way He would pick out anything in style. Clothes and God just don't mix. Are these your thoughts? I know they're the thoughts of many girls out there, but even worse, I know that many other girls out there don't even stop to think about it. They're oblivious to the fact that, *yes*, dressing in a certain way *can* cause destruction—in ways that many girls may not even be aware of.

MEANS OF DESTRUCTION
The weapons are very powerful

1 Corinthians 10:32, "Do not cause anyone to stumble..." (NIV)

So, to end the suspense, the destruction that girls can cause when we don't dress modestly is to – surprise! – guys. The guy sitting behind you in first period. The guys walking past you in the hallway. Your younger brother's friends. The guys you hang out with on the weekend. Your boyfriend. And the guys that you sit next to in the pew on Sunday. Satan works harder and harder every day to destroy their minds and every inch of their purity. He is very familiar with the female longing to be wanted and attractive and He uses the way we girls dress to trick us into thinking that dressing to be noticed is the answer to our heart's desire. But in fact, Satan turns it around so that by the time we're finished trying, 1) we're still empty inside and 2) he's already done his work by violating various guys' hearts and minds. Satan is using the way girls in this generation dress to get a hold of the minds of the male population everywhere, seeking to steal every last drop of their innocence. The result of Satan's tactics? Guys with lustful eyes, lustful hearts, and lustful thoughts that we could have helped prevent in the first place.

It's not our fault! We don't make the fashions! Guys are always thinking about sex, anyways. We have no control over their thoughts—we'll dress however we want. It's the guy's fault if he chooses to think of what's underneath our clothes just because he almost gets a full-on glimpse.

Wrong. As young women, we have a *huge* responsibility to guys, a responsibility that often goes underestimated. When we dress in a way to seduce or lure a guy on to sexual thoughts, it is our fault. When we purposely dress in clothes that we are fully aware are going to make a guy look twice, we are at fault. We are ignoring the responsibility and pretending not to dress that way on purpose, pretending that, oops! you didn't even realize half your back was showing!

I think too often we just blame guys for being a guys and we get this general picture in our heads that, secretly, all guys are these sick perverts that can't keep their minds out of the gutter. We might also assume that just because a guy is in church, he's not going to have any problems with lust. It's not fair to guys at all to make those assumptions. Number one, a guy is a guy and his hormones are going to function the same whether he's singing in the church choir or looking at pornography. Number two, it may be true that guys usually think about sex more than girls, but as sisters in Christ, that's no reason for us to make it all the more hard for guys to remain pure in heart and mind. We complain about guys being "perverted" but we don't do anything to stop it! When we wear shorts that are practically riding up our butts or shirts that practically show everything when we bend over, we're being completely ignorant of our God-given responsibility and in the meantime we cause our brothers to stumble away from purity, and cause those perverted thoughts that we pretend just formed in their minds out of nowhere.

Think about it. When you purposely wear something that you know will make a guy's head turn and his mouth drool, you're causing him to commit adultery against his future wife. It might sound extreme, but look at Matthew 5:28: "But I tell you that anyone who looks at a woman lustfully has already committed adultery with her in his heart." (NIV) Although your future husband probably doesn't know who you are yet, or even if he does, he has a responsibility to remain pure in heart before he gets married (and after, too). But how can he be faithful to you in that way when girls all around him aren't doing anything to help him out and lift him up? When we do the opposite and dress immodestly, willing to show ourselves off in every way, it's like we're going against girls everywhere, encouraging their future husbands to go ahead and think impure thoughts about us, something the future wives would be very hurt with.

Would you want your future husband forming all sorts of impurities in his heart and mind in his head about other girls? I wouldn't, and I doubt you would either. That's why we as a generation of young women have to take on this responsibility more seriously. God is trusting us to do this because He knows that it's not an impossible, or even horrible task. It's a part of being a girl, and a part of God's purpose for your life.

— — —

I'll Say it Again
I'm not finished presenting my case

Haven't convinced you yet? Are you still thinking, *It is not that big a deal! I have the right to dress how I want. Besides, I still don't like the word modesty. It sounds like long dresses and bonnets—something I won't be wearing anytime soon, thank you.*

If you're still a little skeptical of the whole modesty thing, ask yourself this question: *Why do I get dressed in the morning, anyways?*

Duh! I get dressed so I'm not walking around naked! OK, so that would be the obvious answer to the first question. But have you ever thought about dressing as something you do to glorify God in your life? It may seem like something so small and irrelevant to a deep and spiritual relationship with God, but it's not. As Christians, our goal in life should be to bring glory to God in every single thing we do, whether it's as small as getting dressed in the morning or deciding whether or not to have sex before marriage.

It does not bring God glory when we dress to show off our bodies. I don't care if God gave you the longest, skinniest legs out there—you still aren't bringing God glory if you only cover six inches of them! However, it does bring glory to God when we dress in a way that we know will not cause a guy's mind to stumble. I think if we really love God with all of our hearts, we would willingly put forth the effort to glorify Him in this way, as small as it may seem.

I think there are two big reasons why girls dress for attention that relate to things I've talked about earlier: 1) they're trying to fill their void with a guy's attention that actually only God can fill and 2) they have a poor self-image in the first place and they want to get a guy to affirm the way they look to boost their confidence (Satan's trap of affirmation). I think that's why it's so important that we make sure we set those things straight in our lives—filling the void with Christ's love and realizing who we are in Him and how He sees us. When these two parts of our lives are in the wrong place and out of harmony with God's thinking, it's going to be a lot easier for us to immediately give in to the temptation to dress immodestly to satisfy that desire to fill our emptiness or get an extra boost of self-confidence that comes from a whistling guy.

When you get down to it, it's all about remembering Who we're living for, like Paul did back when I was talking about contentment. He kept the finish line in mind and He never forgot Who gave him each breath, and Who saved him from death. And he always remembered Who it was he was trying to bring glory to: God. When we remember that our ultimate goal in life is to please God and listen to His commands for our lives, it will become an easier thing to bring honor to God when we're choosing the clothes that we wear. And don't forget His two greatest commands: loving Him first and then loving others as we love ourselves. The biggest way to bring God honor when we choose what clothes to buy is choosing clothes that will protect the minds of our brothers in Christ. When we dress this way, it is an outward expression of our love for our Savior!

Dressing modestly is also an outward expression of our love for others, as it helps to protect the guys around, Christian or not, from impurity. Dressing to cause a guy to stumble is not loving at all and goes against God's second greatest commandment. Do we love God? Do we have a passion for His purpose? Is our heart's desire really to follow and please Him? If these things are true, then we will have the love of God in our hearts for others and act on it.

So can we dress modestly while still looking stylish and cute? Of course! Trust me, it's possible! The cutest clothes are not always butt-hugging, midriff-baring and cleavage-exposing. Remember, there's nothing wrong with wearing something cute and looking nice. When we're put together in an outfit we really feel good in we feel more confident and there's nothing wrong with that. We just have to stay responsible and be honest when we get ready to go out. Besides, I'm sure I'm not the only one to think that way-too-tight shirts and supershort minis don't look all that cute and flattering anyways. I would much rather be more covered up while flattering my body shape at the same time in a proper way.

Are you willing to let God take control of this area in your life? Are you going to prove trustworthy to God by fighting for the purity of heart and mind of your brothers in Christ? Are you willing to go against the flow of culture and dress to honor God?

– – –

My Own Thoughts

_____

_____

_____

_____

Ask yourself these questions and be honest in your answers:
- *Who am I dressing for?*
- *Are there any outfits in my closet that I bought just to get a guy's attention?*
- *Am I willing to get rid of those outfits to honor God?*
- *Is the way I'm dressing now honoring to God?*
- *Have I been taking my responsibility too lightly?*

CONFESSIONS OF A GIRL

- *Why do I dress the way I dress?*
- *Do I have a poor self-image or has God not filled my void, and if so, is it affecting the way I dress?*
- *How can I honor God better when I'm choosing what to buy?*

A Quick Recap
Modesty in a nutshell

- In today's world, young women are not encouraged to dress modestly, but rather to look as "sexy" as possible.
- We as young women and girls are told to dress modestly in 1 Timothy 2:9 and we can be sure that God put that in His word for a reason.
- Whether we believe it or not, we *are* responsible to God *and* to guys for what we wear.
- We have the power in our hands to either cause a guy to think lustful thoughts or to encourage a guy to keep his mind pure and we are to use that responsibility to do the latter—out of a love for God and out of the love for our neighbors that God commanded us to possess.
- We can actually view dressing as a way to honor God and bring Him glory—or we can use it to dishonor Him.
- Dressing modestly doesn't mean dressing unattractively, but it means dressing in a way that won't cause a guy to stumble; you can dress modestly and still look stylish!
- We have to remember who we're living for and what our main goal in life is.
- Raise the bar....

Chapter 8

It's All In The Mind: God's Greater Calling To Purity On The Inside

2 Corinthians 7:1, "…let's make a clean break with everything that defiles or distracts us, both within and without. Let's make our entire lives fit and holy temples for the worship of God." (Msg)

Colossians 3:2, "Set your minds on things above, not on earthly things." (NIV)

"Um, hey, Mom? Heather's having her birthday party next week and guess what? We're going to see *Titanic*! I can go, right?"

And that is how one of the very first battles (there's too many to count!) over movies with my poor mom began. They'd continue over the next few years, some worse than others.

"Um, yeah, I think so. But you have to walk out of the theatre for those two scenes that I didn't let you see two weeks ago when the family went to see it."

"Mom! You're kidding, right? I am *not* going to just walk out of the theatre! That's so lame!"

"Well, you're not going to watch those scenes!"

"Can't I just close my eyes during those parts? Besides, I know when they're about to come."

"Well…"

"Mom! Be realistic. Do you know how stupid I'd look actually getting up and leaving for those two parts? Everyone would think I was so weird!"

"OK! You can close your eyes. And you *better* close your eyes. I'm going trust you, Tessa."

End of story. If I remember right I didn't actually close my eyes for the entire time but I casually looked around, avoiding the screen, and hid behind my box of candy, pretending to concentrate very hard on what color Sour Patch Kid was about to come out. *No one else's mom made them look away for these scenes! My mom is just too strict about the whole movie thing!*

Does this remind you at all about the whole clothing arguments I had with my mom that I was talking about earlier? Well, we didn't just have arguments about clothes. We fought over and over about movies, TV, and even some music.

The very first time my mom had to put her foot down was when I was probably seven or eight years old. I remember the day very clearly. I was sitting in the TV room and my mom came in to break the terrible news: "Tessa, you're not allowed to watch *Saved by the Bell* anymore." What! Are you kidding me? I watch it every single day! It was the worst thing my mom could have said to me that day. I eventually got over it, but when I'd go over to a friend's house that watched *Saved by the Bell* I got my first chances at passing the test. "I'm uh, not allowed to watch this show…" It seems funny today that my mom would want me to stop watching such a "harmless" show, but I guess at the time she thought I was too young to be watching shows about "grown up high school-aged teenagers." I guess it would have been *pretty* mature content for my little mind back then, or so my mom thought.

When I turned the big thirteen in sixth grade, for some reason I thought I could get off the hook and see a lot more movies. Ha. I was wrong. My parents had decided that they weren't going to let their girls see just anything out there. They were stricter than most parents I knew. Only on very rare occasions would they even allow themselves to watch an R-rated movie.

It was pretty hard for me as I went through my junior high years. Although my mom loosened up a little bit, she still stood her ground most of the time and did not let me see several movies. And then there was the time when she just had to discover this sneaky little website online that gave every single detail about a new movie in the theatres. Every cuss word. Every drink of alcohol. Every glance of cleavage. To me it was the website from hell.

Time and again I'd have to tell my friends, "Well...sorry, but I'm not allowed to see it," and then grumble under my breath about my mom's rules being so stupid. I could really be the biggest brat sometimes to my mom while we were arguing. I know that sometimes I got into such a fit that I'm sure my mom just didn't want to argue anymore and let her guard down and hesitantly let me see a movie after I begged and begged. When I look back, I wish I hadn't given my mom all that trouble. I'm just glad she didn't let me win very often.

"But Mom! So and so's mom is letting her see it!"

Can you guess what the answer was almost every time? I think almost every teenager on this planet has heard it at least once.

"But I'm not so and so's mom, am I?"

"Uggghhh!"

I should have just predicted the answer and saved some energy.

It's funny that I'm writing this chapter right now because just tonight my sister had to go through one of these familiar battles herself. She just turned fifteen so she's right around very prime age for the kind of thing I'm talking about. Her friends were going to see a movie that just came out and of course my mom turned to her trusty little website. She didn't like what she saw, and neither did my dad when he looked at it. In the end, my sister lost the battle (which was actually a calmer battle than some of the others I've seen) and she wasn't allowed to go to the movie. I could identify with her anger over the decision so much because I knew exactly how she felt—I felt the very same way when I was her age. I wonder when she's going to have a change of heart? *I wonder when she's going to realize that mom is on her side?* It definitely took me a while to realize that fact.

It got harder for me in 7th grade when we girls finally started realizing that we wanted to hang out with the guys on the weekends. No more "girls only" get-togethers. First came guy/girl birthday parties, which were such a huge deal, and then we actually stared *going places* with the guys. We thought it was a pretty big thing. Anyways, there were times when I'd think to myself, *if the guys find out I'm not allowed to see this movie they're really going to think I'm dumb. I wish my parents would just let up a little.*

I thought my own parents were strict until I got to know my (now) best friend Jillian. At first, she wasn't even allowed to see almost anything PG-13. *I wonder if Jillian gets as mad as I do about not being able to see so many movies? I wonder if Jillian and her mom have countless little arguments over ratings and sex scenes and profanity?* I'm sure they did. Nonetheless,

IT'S ALL IN THE MIND: GOD'S GREATER CALLING TO PURITY ON THE INSIDE

finding out that I wasn't the only one with strict parents was a little encouraging to me. Sometimes it even made me feel better to know that there were some parents out there that were stricter than mine!

If only I had been mature enough to be thankful for my mom's protectiveness back then. I think deep down inside I knew that it was for the better that she was trying to keep me from filling my mind with junk, but of course at the time I felt like she was being overprotective.

I don't know the exact time when God began to work in my heart about this issue, but I think it was sometime during 8th grade. God challenged me a lot that year. One Friday night a group of people from school were going to see a movie. I can't even remember my mom's opinion about my going to see it, but she probably said something like, "Well...I don't really *want* you to see it, but I'm going to leave it to your own personal conviction. It's between you and God." All I can remember is being more convinced than usual that night and feeling as though I shouldn't go. The movie they were going to see wasn't full of sex scenes, totally overloaded with profanity, or even violent. (I had looked it up on the website. Yes...I was turning to the website that I once thought of as the enemy!) It was your typical comedy with profanity here and there, sexual humor, etc.

I remember talking to my one friend when we were in the middle of trying to finalize the plans (who would drive us, what time, etc.) and telling her that I didn't think I wanted to go.

"What!? Why?"

"I, um...I don't really think...it's something I want to see..." I tried my best to sound cool, like I knew what I was talking about, all the while knowing I probably sounded stupid to my friend. After all, it was just a PG-13 movie, nothing *horrible*. Besides, the friends I was going with were friends from my *Christian* school. Certainly it wasn't that big a deal, was it? God knew it was impossible to go to a movie where there was no cussing at all didn't He? God realized that it was just the norm for something sexual to be in every comedy, every drama, every action movie, (and especially!) every romance, right? Surely God didn't expect us to just not go to the movies! Talk about taking Christianity to the extreme!

I wrestled with thoughts like these over and over. Where exactly are Christians supposed to stand when it comes to entertainment—movies, music, TV shows, etc.? Where does God draw the line? Do we have to listen to Christian music only? Do we have to watch only PG-rated movies? The world around me was waging a war against me. Here I came to another battle, possibly the hardest of them all.

— — —

The Way We're Entertained
Society is looking for D-R-A-M-A

I remember very clearly when the popular game show featuring Regis Philbin, *Who Wants to be a Millionaire,* aired for the first season. America hadn't seen a game show like it ever before. I remember watching it one Friday night up in my parents' room and cheering for the first guy on the show to win one million dollars. Now *that* was something America had never seen before—and it was exciting! In a sense, *Who Wants to be a Millionaire* was America's first very popular reality TV show, at least that's where I think it began. Maybe it began with MTV's *The Real World*. I guess no one can say for sure. Whatever the case, people liked it because it dealt with real people. It wasn't done from a script, and it was very entertaining.

IT'S ALL IN THE MIND: GOD'S GREATER CALLING TO PURITY ON THE INSIDE

The entertainment industry instantly took notice of *Who Wants to be a Millionaire's* popular ratings and all the attention it was getting. Before America could even blink, reality TV shows were popping up all over the place. It was something new for entertainment-seekers and they seemed to love it. I remember the first few reality TV shows. There was the widely popular show *Survivor*, where adults of all ages were forced to live in some exotic place and "survive" from being kicked out by their fellow teammates to win one million dollars while also trying to survive the tough living conditions. And then there was *The Bachelor* – the show where a real-life bachelor got to choose from about twenty different women to marry. And who can forget the first season of *American Idol* or *Fear Factor*?

Over the last three years it seems as though almost every popular TV show (besides *Friends* and *The O.C.*) is a reality show. Society has fallen in love with drama. We don't even care anymore if a so-called reality TV show is rumored to be staged. We tell ourselves the drama is real, and we spend countless hours watching it–whether it's *Who Wants to Marry my Dad?* or *Trading Spouses*. If there's drama, if there's conflict, if there's steamy romance, if there's something we've never seen before, we want it.

So, by now it might seem like I'm totally bashing reality TV. I don't want you to think that, because not all reality TV is bad. I just wanted to make the point that our society is in love with drama and conflict. We love to see people engaging in it. When we feel like our lives are too simple and nothing good is ever going on, we can just turn on the TV and find someone in a much more "exciting" situation and put ourselves right there with them, cheering them on or booing them off the show.

It seems that somewhere over the years society got totally bored with innocent, yet entertaining shows such as the two once popular TV shows *Full House and Family Matters* that once ruled Friday night primetime. At one point, decency became boring and producers felt the pressure to turn it up a notch on the sexual content and the profane dialogue. After a while it became normal to watch a TV show and hear a cuss word every now and then. As I write this, something that should be an issue but isn't one is the casualness of homosexual characters on primetime sitcoms. There are even some reality TV shows that glorify homosexuality—a sin that God clearly and strongly speaks against in His word. (See 1 Corinthians 6:9) Yet it's becoming a common thing to see in today's entertainment, as it's pushing harder and harder to be accepted by society.

I could go on for pages to describe vulgarity seen and heard in movies, music, and primetime sitcoms that are everywhere today, but I'm not going to because we all know it's there without having to have every detail explained to us. We're all aware of the large amount of sexual content, the swiftly rising amount of nudity, the glorification of wealth (especially on reality TV), the outrageous amount of profanity, the tolerance of sins that God speaks directly against in His word, and so on. It's everywhere and I don't see it leaving anytime soon. Unless perhaps we stand up against it.

— — —

SATAN'S MEANS OF ATTACK
They're up against God's quiet, yet powerful whisper

In the midst of such a powerful entertainment industry, with Satan working behind the scenes, I believe that something horrible has happened to Christians, something that we may not even be aware of. We have let ourselves completely blend in with society's style of entertainment. In another sense, we've become friends with the world's entertainment. There's hardly a way to tell the difference anymore between many Christians and non-Christians if you observe what they watch and listen to. I feel that, unfortunately, Christians have jumped on the entertainment bandwagon and have forgotten Jesus' precious command in 1 John 2:19:

"Do not love the world or anything in the world…" (NIV)

Over the past couple of years, God has spoken to me a great deal about raising the bar on what I let my eyes see and my ears hear—two things that greatly affect what goes on in my heart and my mind. God has quietly yet firmly whispered to me, "Tessa…I want more from you *right now*. I don't care how much you're going to stand out. I don't care what your friends are going to think of you. I want you to glorify Me in *every single thing you do*. I want you to build a higher standard when it comes to what you feed your mind!"

I had to get over the concern of whether or not I was going to look cool to my friends. I had to get over the fact that I might be made fun of—even by some of my Christian friends, which was probably the hardest thing of all. I had to get over the fact that people were probably going to think I was just trying to look better than them or that I was trying to be a "snobby church girl," which, yes, someone has called me before.

Sometimes I'd ask myself if I was taking things too much to the extreme. After all, I knew that a lot of respected Christians that I really looked up to were watching R-rated movies on the weekends, so it was hard for me to determine if I really had my head on straight. Was I just trying too hard to be a perfect saint in a world of imperfect sinners? Did God really care that much about what I watched and listened to as long as it wasn't really, really bad? Was just "sort of bad" OK with God?

God continued to whisper to me, "No. I want more from you. Raise the bar, Tessa. Don't settle for a mediocre relationship with Me. Set the standard higher for Christians. Run the race with a greater determination, run it with every ounce of strength you have. Don't settle for average. Don't settle for lukewarm. There is so much more out there than that and I want you to find it. And if you truly want to find it, you're going to have to purify yourself from every form of evil in this world—every form of worldly entertainment that will cause you to have impure thoughts, worldly motives, selfish ambitions, and a mindset that is anything away from My own."

God made Himself clear to me, and I strongly believe that if this generation wants to make any changes, wants to make any difference at all, and wants to fulfill any of God's purposes, we have to stop being so lukewarm in our relationships with God when it comes to movies, TV, music, and the like. We have to listen to His voice and do every single thing in our will to remain pure in heart and mind before His eyes. Because guess what? God isn't looking for Christians that halfway honor Him. God doesn't want us living in the gray. He's looking for a simple "yes" or a "no." Black or white.

I hesitate on expanding on this topic for fear that you might think I'm sounding preachy, or worse, like your mom. But I'm going to try to get over that fear real quick here because I definitely have more to say. So think whatever you wish of my opinion, love me or hate me for it, but at least read it. Because I can't keep this inside of me any longer.

IT'S ALL IN THE MIND: GOD'S GREATER CALLING TO PURITY ON THE INSIDE

Earlier in the book I quoted Revelation 3:15, but I want you to look at it again. It says, "I know your deeds, that you are neither cold nor hot. I wish you were either one or the other!" (NIV) Without a question, God's first choice is for us to be "hot" and on fire in our relationship with Him. But can you believe that God would rather we be ice cold in our relationship with Him than just warm like bath water that's already been sitting still for ten minutes? It's true. God is looking for more than the "fired-up" Christian that still mindlessly watches whatever movie he or she feels like on the weekends. God wants *all* of you or He wants nothing.

Going along with and engaging in the world's ways of entertainment is just one way that Christians have caused themselves to fall into a stale, lukewarm relationship with God—a relationship that lacks passion, complete surrender, and abandonment of the world. And one thing I know for sure is that God is calling on us to raise the bar in this area of our lives. I feel that Christians in this generation have become too oblivious to the thousands of ways that Satan is using the entertainment industry to hinder them from reaching their utmost potential in their relationship with Christ. Satan is seeking every day to destroy the hearts and minds of Christians, and I strongly believe that his biggest target is young people.

The pressure is on for us to look cool around our friends. We're expected to know everything about the latest movies, singers, bands, and TV shows. The media gives an enormous amount of glorification to these things and young people are expected to love them, enjoy them, take interest in them, talk about them, and know all the facts about them.

But you see, this creates a problem. Because when we open ourselves up to the media and all that it supposedly has for us, it's like we instantly open the door for Satan. We're allowing him to come into our lives and walk all over our hearts and minds, using the world's entertainment to appear as something normal and innocent that every "average teen" – Christian or not – takes part in. It's like we're unintentionally saying to Satan, "Come on in and stay a while. Take off your coat and make yourself comfortable." And we can be sure that Satan will never, ever ignore an invitation like that. He waits for those invitations day and night.

So what exactly do I mean by opening the door for Satan to come in? What I mean is, when we engage in entertaining ourselves with things that have even a hint of impurity or worldliness in them, we immediately give Satan a foothold over what we think about and what goes on in our hearts. If you watch or listen to something that repeats the "F" word ten times, Satan is going to pound that word into your head and make you think of it over and over, even though you try to ignore it when you hear it every ten minutes in a movie or every five lines in the lyrics to a song. When we watch a TV show that displays a character with an angry and rebellious attitude, Satan will do everything in his power to try and make that attitude rub off on us or to appear cool to us, something that we want to copy. And the more often we allow Satan that foothold in our lives, the easier it's going to be for him to attack us. Now look at the way Satan uses what I believe to be our two most important senses – hearing and seeing – to strike us in the mind and in the heart; two places that control a great deal of how we go about living our everyday lives.

— — —

IT'S ALL IN THE MIND: GOD'S GREATER CALLING TO PURITY ON THE INSIDE

My Thoughts

_____

_____

_____

_____

_____

_____

– – –

SATAN'S ATTACK ON THE MIND
How Satan uses entertainment to get a foothold on our thoughts

Philippians 4:8, "Finally, brothers, whatever is true, whatever is noble, whatever is right, whatever is pure, whatever is lovely, whatever is admirable – if anything is excellent or praiseworthy – think about such things." (NIV)

So many things go on inside of my head—weird thoughts, crazy thoughts, judgmental thoughts, mean thoughts, peaceful thoughts (those I like the most!), happy thoughts, and sometimes, impure thoughts. My mind is a monster of a million thoughts throughout the day, ranging anywhere from very good to very bad. My thoughts are something that I have struggled a very great deal with over the years. Many times I've been ashamed of the things that I'm thinking, and many times I've been thinking of something and then I've asked myself, *What if someone could read your mind? What if your thoughts were posted for a whole group of people that were close to you to see?* Many times the answer would be, *I'd be humiliated! People would think I was the strangest person on earth! Some people would probably even hate me. People would lose some of their respect for me.* Other times I'd answer to myself, *People probably wouldn't understand me at all! My thoughts are too deep and way out there, even I don't understand them sometimes!*

Our thoughts are so personal and "hidden" from the world, yet Satan knows how powerful they can be when used against us. He knows how much they can damage our relationship with Christ. He knows that our thoughts can hinder us from keeping the mindset of Christ and distract us from thinking about the things that Christ would have us think about, so He deceivingly persuades us to fill our minds with junk and tries to tell us that we're not harming ourselves at all. But the truth of the matter is that whatever we put into our minds through entertainment, it's going to be reflected back into our thoughts. If we watch movies with a bunch of sex scenes or even sexual humor, our minds are going to capture those things and remind us of them later. Impure sexual thoughts can often times turn to lustful thoughts towards the opposite sex that can cause us to sin against God and even our future spouses (see Matthew 5:28 again!). It might be a common thing to think that guys are the only ones that deal with lust, but it's not true. Girls deal with lust a great deal as well. Watching a TV show that glorifies a guy's body or watching a sex scene where a guy is half naked can definitely lead to lust in a girl's heart and mind.

Listening to music that continually talks about sexual relationships will also get a hold of our mind, especially when we find we have the song stuck in our heads and we can't quit repeating the lyrics over and over again. The words can also cause us to visualize what the song is talking about, which can really put our thoughts on the wrong track.

Sexual scenes and dialogue have almost become a normal part of entertainment, and I know that they are affecting so many young people out there who struggle daily with keeping their thoughts pure. That is why I think we have to work harder to stay away from the sources of these thoughts. Just throwing out one CD that you know contributes to impure thoughts can make a great deal of difference.

Something else that is becoming even more common in entertainment that affects our thoughts a great deal and that Satan has been having the time of his life with is the profane language that we hear over and over and over. I've seen more than one PG-13 movie that could easily have gotten a PG rating if it weren't for the language. Did someone one day declare that PG movies were uncool? Did someone decide that it was impossible to make a box office hit without using profanity? It seems to me like that is the case. It's as though the director believes that the more trash in a movie, the more it will sell, which sadly in a few cases is probably true. But it's definitely not always the case. There have been plenty of times that I've seen a PG movie do so much better at the box office than a PG-13 movie full of profanity. Some of the best-selling recording artists have never even added one swear word to their lyrics. Yet some still believe that it's what makes something entertaining, so they add at least three into every scene, at least one into every episode, and at least two into every song. I'd bet you a million bucks that these songs and TV shows and movies would sell just as well if the profanity were taken out. The majority of people don't engage in any sort of entertainment to listen to all the expletives. People are looking for a good plot, something to laugh at, a good tune with a good beat, and lyrics that really mean something—all things that can easily be accomplished without the profane language.

Listening to the profanity over and over again will do two things to us: 1) it will cause us to think those words to ourselves more often, even if we don't say them out loud, and 2) it will cause us to eventually become desensitized to profanity which is actually very dangerous to our Christian walk.

When we become desensitized to something, it doesn't bother us anymore. It's very easy to become desensitized to something when you're around it all the time. Unfortunately, we can't always control what we hear from the people around us. I remember when I switched from the small Christian school that I had attended from Kindergarten to eighth grade, to a public school in ninth grade. Instantly I realized that I was surrounded by ten times the amount of profanity I was hearing on a daily basis before. It was very "ear-opening" for me to be around that all the time and I found that eventually those words popped into my mind more easily and they became something normal for me to hear. I'd find myself almost slipping more often when I got angry and shouting one of them out or even mumbling one under my breath. It's different from having a friend that you can ask not to swear around you, to hearing it from various people talking to their friends (or in some cases their enemies) when you're just innocently walking through the hallways.

So obviously there are definitely going to be times where we can't get away from hearing all "those words," but why do we make it worse for ourselves by allowing ourselves to hear those words from things that we can control? Why do we sit around and allow things that we can control to enter our minds and affect the way we think? I think we often underestimate the power of what we hear. We casually assume

IT'S ALL IN THE MIND: GOD'S GREATER CALLING TO PURITY ON THE INSIDE

that we'll forget about it or be able to effortlessly let it go in one ear and out the other. But it simply doesn't work that way. Our minds will always have a way of remembering what we hear, especially when we're hearing it over and over again.

Paying little attention to what we watch and listen to can also affect us deeper than our minds; it can affect the purity of the things that go on in our hearts—our motives, our ambitions, and our attitudes our desires. When we open these things up to the corrupt ways of the world, they're going to go from unpolluted to tainted and worldly, far from the beauty and nature of Christ, the two things that genuine Christians work hard to reflect out of pure love for their Savior.

Perhaps we too often feel that it doesn't matter what we think about or what goes on inside our hearts because no one else can see it. As long as we appear to be decent Christians on the outside, we'll gain the respect we're looking for. Well it may be true that no one on earth can read our minds, but every single one of our thoughts and every single thing that goes on inside of our hearts can never be hidden from God—it's impossible. Every time we think something impure, God sees it. Every time our hearts are filled with selfish ambitions, God sees it. Hebrews 4:13 says, "Nothing at all is hidden from God's sight. Everything is uncovered and laid bare before the eyes of Him to whom we must give account." (NIV) How often we have failed to understand the importance of this verse! First of all, if it exists, God sees it! Second of all, we have to give an account for every impure thought, every wrongful attitude, every lustful eye, and every worldly desire. We're not going to get away with them, and we cannot hide them from God.

God knew that we were going to be tempted to fill our minds with every immoral thing that came our way—even if it seemed totally innocent to us. He knew the power of Satan would be strong and He knew that Satan was going to try to deceive us into thinking it didn't matter what entertainment we filled our lives with. And that is why His word tells us in Philippians 4:8, "Finally, brothers, whatever is true, whatever is noble, whatever is right, whatever is pure, whatever is lovely, whatever is admirable – if anything is excellent or praiseworthy – think about such things." (NIV)

I also love how this verse is translated in *The Message*, "Summing it all up, friends, I'd say you'll do best by filling your minds and meditating on things true, noble, reputable, authentic, compelling, gracious—the best, not the worst; the beautiful, not the ugly; things to praise, not to curse."

God's desire for our lives is to fill our minds with the truth, things that are *authentic, genuine, and real*. Things that are upright and honorable. We simply cannot fulfill this area of God's purpose for our lives if we continue to go on living the average Christian life, "innocently" listening to music that goes against the word of God and basically is the complete opposite of His nature. We cannot keep telling ourselves that "one song won't hurt," because pretty soon "ten songs won't hurt." We can't keep debating every weekend whether or not we're going to go see a movie full of profanity and sex and violence and then at the last minute decide that it won't affect us and that there's nothing else to see. In simple terms, we cannot keep settling for the normal Christian life. Too many Christians are settling for a lukewarm commitment to God in the area of entertainment and if we want to raise the bar at all in our generation we're going to have to pay more attention to this problem.

Let me tell you, this part of the book isn't easy for me to write, because it's probably one of the touchiest subjects I could have come up with. I know that Christians have a lot of different viewpoints on where to draw the line with

IT'S ALL IN THE MIND: GOD'S GREATER CALLING TO PURITY ON THE INSIDE

entertainment, and I know that my viewpoint is probably one of the most extreme of them. I don't really care though because God has been convincing me over and over again to raise the bar in this area and I couldn't have spilled out the rest of my heart in this book without touching on it. If you want to roll your eyes at me and call me your mom, be my guest. But *listen* to God's voice in this area of your life. Does He want more of you? Is He asking you to be more disciplined? Is He asking you to make more sacrifices, not caring what people think? Is He asking you to speak up more? Don't ignore Him.

You might be thinking to yourself that I'm suggesting something totally boring and a totally lame way of life, but all I'm asking is for you to, again, remember Who you're living for. Remember Who you're supposed to be living to please and bring glory to–God and not the world. And remember why–not because you want to be a saint, not because you want to be the perfect Christian, not because you want to look better than everyone else around you, but because you love Him, and you want to fulfill His purpose in your life. Because you would rather give up everything in this world to see His face. Because you're so in awe of who He is that you desire nothing more than to please Him. Make that be your reason for keeping your mind pure and filtering out what goes into your mind.

Well, you might as well ask us to live the most boring life on earth! Hardly. I'm asking you to live the most exciting life on earth–the most rewarding, the most abundant, the most beautiful life you can imagine. Do you never lie in bed at night and wonder, *Is this all that the world has to offer me?* Stop wondering because, yes, what you see around you is what the world has to offer you: the sexual immorality, the pain, the selfishness, the violence, the spiteful attitudes. But it is not what God has to offer you. He has so much more, so many more wonderful things, things that offer truth and hope and peace. We just have to seek them with all our hearts and close the door to the world around us.

We have to make some changes in this area of our lives—if not now, when will we? I'm pleading with myself and I'm pleading with you; raise the bar higher and work harder at filtering out what goes into your mind. God will see that and He will honor you for that. The cost on earth is temporary, but the reward in Heaven is eternal.

My Thoughts
Is there anything that you need to begin filtering out of your lifestyle? Music? Movies? TV shows? Do you honestly feel that you're honoring God and bringing glory to Him with everything you watch and listen to? If not, what changes need to be made and why are these changes important to you? Is your number one desire to please God no matter what that may make you look like to your friends?

_____

_____

_____

_____

_____

Chapter 9

A Hope And A Future: Learning To Trust God With The Puzzle Of Life

Jeremiah 29:11, "'For I know the plans I have for you', declares the LORD, 'plans to prosper you and not to harm you, plans to give you a hope and a future.'" (NIV)

Your parents started asking you when you were somewhere around five years old. Your first grade teacher asked you, along with your second grade teacher, and probably even your third grade teacher. Your answers were either completely different every time you were asked or every time the answer was exactly the same as you stated it with great confidence and assurance. It's the question that causes the imagination to run wildly and it's the question that causes us to envision a million different possibilities. It's the question that provides the possible answer to our entire future. It's the question that we'll answer when we're picking out a college and it's the question that some adults are still trying to answer. And lastly, it's one of those questions that does not have one right and final answer. Ten simple words to the question, and a million not-so-simple answers.

What do you want to be when you grow up?

I was one of those kids that had the same answer for quite a number of years: a teacher. I loved playing school at home and practically forced my younger sister to sit down and let me "teach" her. (I still take credit today for her learning to read so quickly.) I loved to pretend I was taking attendance and checking whether my "students" wanted plain milk or chocolate-flavored milk for lunch. I loved to think about the day when I could have real students and mark their math books with red stars and smiley faces of approval.

My sister, on the other hand, was a little confused about what she wanted to be. When she was around five or so we asked her what she wanted to be. With all the self-assurance in the world she informed us that when she grew up she wanted to be a "passenger." We secretly laughed at it back then because she obviously had her definitions mixed up, and now we love to remind her of that response whenever the topic comes up. I'm not sure what her next answer was after she learned that she probably wouldn't have any luck trying to earn an income being a passenger. I wonder what picture she had in her mind when she envisioned herself being a passenger?

As I got older, my answers went back and forth. There were some times when I wanted to be an architect, other times when I wanted to be a clothing designer, and at one point I thought I was going to be a lawyer. I had my heart set on going to an Ivy League college such as Yale or Princeton. Let's just say it didn't take too long for me to change my mind on that one. As I got into high school, I began getting even more ideas and became somewhat confused about what I wanted to do because I had so many different interests. Did I still want to teach? If so, what age and what subject? Did I want to go into youth ministry? And what about my two biggest passions, writing and dancing? Was there anything I could do to incorporate those into my career?

Here I am now with one year of high school left and I still don't know what I'm going to major in when I go to college or where the Lord will lead me in a career. But I do know that I have a lot of huge dreams for my future—dreams that I hope will one day be accomplished, God willing. Sometimes I think about my future and wonder just where in the world God is going to take me in the next ten, twenty, and thirty years of my life?

Last summer God really spoke to me about my future when I was going through something that would definitely affect my days to come. My dad had passed a hearing loss condition on to me when I was born. The condition is one that can begin to affect its victim at any age. It didn't begin to affect my dad until he was in his thirties, but it had chosen to affect me by the time I was sixteen. By the end of my sophomore year I had lost a very noticeable amount of hearing and by the end of the summer I could no longer talk on the telephone or go see a movie in the theatre. (If I wanted to catch the whole plot! Which I did…if I was going to spend $7.50!) Conversations with a group of friends were not relaxing and fun for me, but there were times when I found myself just straining to hear as much as I could. I became very self-conscious around crowds and I was constantly worried that someone was trying to talk to me and I couldn't hear them; I was afraid people were getting the idea I was some snob trying to ignore them, when really I just couldn't hear them.

I remember very clearly the day I was working out at a Curves gym, my thoughts nowhere near what I was doing, but far off into the future. A huge dream had popped into my head somewhere between the calf machine and the abs machine and a hundred thoughts began forming in my mind for what I wanted to do when I grew up and I was excitedly filling in all the details of how I wanted it go on. Nothing that might hinder me from realizing this dream came to my mind; my only thought was that I wanted to accomplish it.

I don't know if it was a time when I was feeling discouraged about my hearing (there were many that summer) or if it was just a time where my own "reality" popped into my head, but I remember that dream coming to mind again one day soon after that "awakening" in the gym and I stopped dead in my tracks and thought to myself: *Hellooo! You can't accomplish that dream or any other dreams you've been having with your hearing loss. To do the things that you want to do you have to be able to hear.* I was completely devastated. I felt hopeless and without a future. It hadn't really registered before. How could I dance if the words to the songs were all jumbled together to form an annoying sound amidst a tune that my ears couldn't set straight? How could I teach if I couldn't hear my students ask me questions? It was questions like these that instantly raced through my mind and suddenly a wave of worry rushed through me. Was I going to be jobless? How was I going to support myself when I was fresh out of college and in need of a career?

God must have been up in heaven wondering when in the world did I take my eyes off His promises in the Bible—promises that He would never leave me and promises that He had a plan for my life? But He was quietly and patiently waiting to reveal something to me that I want to share with the rest of my generation. I think it's an issue that usually isn't even thought of as an "issue"—something obvious that we deal with, such as the things I've gone over previously, relationships, self-image, etc. I think it's something that a lot of us hold deep inside ourselves, not wanting others to see it. The issue is worry—worry about the future in particular.

Some of you are in situations that make it really hard for you to get into the college you'd need to go to in order to receive an education in something that you're certain you want to pursue, possibly because the tuition cost is just too high. Some of you are in situations where you can't go to college at all because you have to take over the family business or the money just isn't there. Maybe your life situation in general makes it impossible for you to have the *time* to go to college. Maybe there are some of you thinking the thoughts that I did only a year ago and you feel as though there is no way possible for you to achieve what you want in life. And then there are some of you who just have no idea *what* you want to do in the future and the time to choose seems to be rapidly sneaking up on you. To some of you these situations have created feelings of hopelessness, perhaps even despair. To some of you these situations may make you feel like failures or "nobodies" without a future.

I believe that my generation has lost a "sense of purpose" in life and that we've been settling for a passionless existence and "average" plans for the future. We've let go of God's promises that He has laid out for us in His word and have casually begun to downsize our dreams, trying our best to keep "reality" in mind.

But...God looks at our situations from a different viewpoint. In Isaiah 55:8-9 the Bible says, "'I don't think the way you think. The way you work isn't the way I work.' God's decree. 'For as the sky soars high above earth, so the way I work surpasses the way you work, and the way I think is beyond the way you think.'" (Msg) In these two verses it's laid out as plain as day to us: we're the humans, God is God. His thoughts are on a way different track than ours. He sees the bigger, *much* bigger, picture. Our plans could be completely different from God's plans. *But I know what I want in life—what if God's plan for me is completely different from what I want?* It's a good question, but I have an even better answer: God's plans for you are the *best* you could ever imagine. Remember, God sees the bigger picture, and what we *think* is right for us now could be completely wrong for us in the future. And God isn't aiming to give us all mediocre jobs that we despise. He isn't setting His sights on giving us a miserable life in the future. Look at what the Bible says in Jeremiah 29:11: "I know what I'm doing. I have it all planned out—plans to take care of you, not abandon you, plans to give you the future you hope for." (Msg)

God obviously wanted to point out to us that He knows what He's doing; every single detail of our lives is in His control and He has an amazing plan for each and every one of us.

I think that a lot of times we get discouraged when we want our lives to follow a very specific track. We plan out our futures year by year and then things suddenly get turned upside down or even go slightly different from what we had planned and we feel as though God set us up for disaster or that He's too busy trying to work out all the details of someone else's life.

I know that there is a lot of hurt and pain and confusion and awful situations out there that cause us to feel this discouragement. But I wonder what would happen if we began to hand our futures over to God and simply *depended* on Him in every aspect of our lives? So many times it's tempting to assume that God has left us alone to figure it out all by ourselves. Take for example, one of the most obvious areas this occurs in: our love lives. We shut God out of this extremely important part of our lives thinking that God couldn't possibly take the time to work out such a "complicated" detail. In the end we desperately try to see the big picture and handle it on our own, hoping we're getting it all right.

I once heard an analogy comparing our lives to a puzzle with hundreds of tiny little pieces, all tiny details that fit perfectly together to form one big picture. Individually the little pieces appear to have no purpose. Some of them look like they don't even fit anywhere in the puzzle at all, but they always do. Some of them can be easily fitted together and others you can't tell where they fit until the end.

The analogy went on to say that we won't ever be able to put the entire puzzle together because we don't have the one, single essential we need: the cover to the puzzle box that displays the finished picture, the guide to fitting the pieces together. Without it, we're clueless as to what the final product should look like. We forget the fact that – guess what? – we're never going to find that box cover. We can search everywhere but we're never going to be able to find it. Why? Because God is the only One who has it. He has *every single* box cover to every *single puzzle* out there. It's kind of weird to picture God up in Heaven holding millions of puzzle boxes, but the analogy works.

Some of us think we don't even need a box cover. We've already given up our laborious search for that crucial guide and we've decided that we can just put the puzzle together without it. It might take a little longer, of course, but we're pretty confident that we'll eventually get it. Hours turn into days, days turn into months, and months turn into years. From the moment we get out of bed to the last waking hour of the day, we're spending all of our time working on that puzzle—but we just can't seem to get it. Once in a while we can find two or three pieces that fit together, but we always come to a dead end and can't ever connect them with the other parts. The labor constantly appears to be pointless and in exasperation we cry out, "What is going on?!"

All of this effort is yet to be proved to be in vain. The puzzle is not going to be figured out. How I long for the day when every young person in my generation comes to the point in his or her life and realizes that the only way to truly live with a purpose and a future is to simply trust that God has it all in His hands. When will the day come when the anxious thoughts disappear and the worry and confusion come to an end? When will this generation realize that every second spent on the search for the box cover is only another second wasted? God has the box cover, and He simply cannot wait to put the pieces together to form the very puzzle that He alone created. We cannot trust in our own efforts to put it together, but we must allow God to orchestrate the details—the ones that appear in good circumstances and bad circumstances, in grief, in pain and in the richest of joys. Worry will only complicate the process and keep us locked away from the beautiful freedom of allowing God to accomplish His plan for our lives.

In Matthew 6:34 the Bible says, "Therefore do not worry about tomorrow, for tomorrow will worry about itself…" (NIV) This is Jesus speaking to every single person and He is not merely *suggesting* that we don't worry but He is *commanding* us not to worry. Worry causes the circumstances of life to appear as though they are about to devour our very souls and it causes us to lose our focus and…sink. It reminds me of the story of Jesus' disciple Peter found in Matthew 14. Peter and the other eleven disciples were out in a boat while Jesus had gone off to pray. Here's the story:

A HOPE AND A FUTURE: LEARNING TO TRUST GOD WITH THE PUZZLE OF LIFE

Meanwhile, the boat was far out to sea when the wind came up against them and they were battered by the waves. At about four o' clock in the morning, Jesus came toward them walking on the water. They were scared out of their wits. "A ghost!" they said, crying out in terror. But Jesus was quick to comfort them. "Courage, it's me. Don't be afraid." Peter, suddenly bold, said, "Master, if it's really you, call me to come to you on the water." He said, "Come ahead." Jumping out of the boat, Peter walked on the water to Jesus. But when he looked down at the waves churning beneath his feet, he lost his nerve and started to sink. He cried, "Master, save me!"
(Matthew 14:24-30, Msg)

Peter heard His loving Savior and Friend calling out to him on the waters and as soon as he recognized Jesus' voice, he excitedly got out of the boat and proceeded to walk on the water—something that most everyone would think to be out of the question and impossible for any mere human to do. The first few steps Peter's eyes were clearly on Jesus – He was pulling off the impossible! – but the moment he forgot that keeping his focus completely on Jesus was the *only* way that could get him across, and as soon as he got distracted and took his eyes off of Jesus, he began to sink. How often in life we do the same thing, one moment trusting that God will get us across the water to achieve the impossible, the unknown, and the next moment we forget that there's no way that our own ability is enough to walk on the water. We slowly turn our focus away from the One Who is calling out for us to come further and further and in an instant we get a glimpse of the circumstances around us and we totally lose hope of the great adventure that we were sure Jesus had called us to.

If only in these times we'd realize that the only way we can walk on water in this life is if we truly know that God and God alone is the only One that can take us across, and that it is imperative that we keep our eyes carefully and steadily focused on the One that enabled us to take our very first step – the Creator of the water, the Creator of gravity, the Creator of man – and the God of the entire universe! He's the only one that can keep us afloat in the midst of the raging waves that in all their strength seek to overcome us in the storms of life. We cannot look down on those waves and immediately think that we alone can get across them. We cannot let the waves batter our souls and put a weight on our shoulders that drags us down into the murky waters, an unforgiving anchor chained to our helpless feet of mere flesh.

Listen to the call. Jesus is eagerly, yet patiently calling out to us, "Come ahead, my child. Come out to the waters and walk with Me. I will take you into the unknown. To man this may seem impossible, but keep in mind that it is I." It is time for this generation to answer God's call for us to follow Him into the unknown where He will take what we thought to be a life full of confusion, fear, worry, and hopelessness, and turn it into a life of hope, a life of achieving the impossible, a life of following dreams, and a life of passion. Are you ready for God to take you into this life? Are you ready to quit working on the puzzle of life—whether you're still looking for the box cover or if you've already given up and are stuck with a bunch of pieces that don't fit together? Wait no longer…

My Thoughts
Have you been searching for the box cover to your puzzle?
Have you been trying to put the puzzle together yourself?
Where has this gotten you?

\- - -

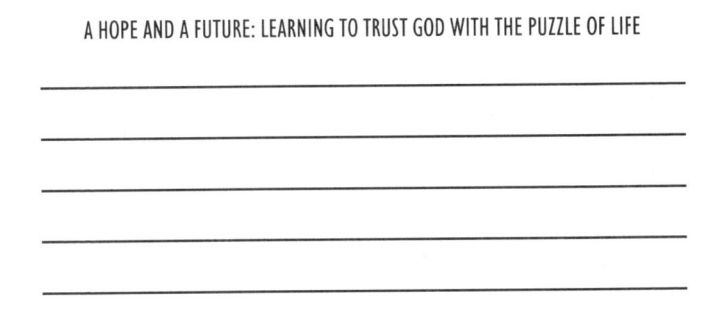

Psalms 46:10, "Be still, and know that I am God;..." (NIV)

Silent stillness is not something that comes easily in a world that is always busy, on the go, and in a hurry. On the road, drivers weave in and out of lanes, honk their horns, tail slow drivers, and occasionally slip the finger to the guy in the car behind them who is making them especially angry. Grocery lines are filled with antsy and anxious people that, by the time they get to the register, are already irritated that they've actually had to wait five minutes longer than they had planned.

I think that hurry and impatience are huge problems we face today. The general attitude of society seems to be "now, now, now" and "for me, me, me." We buzz around like little bees from one place to the next, rarely taking the time to stop and just take *notice* of what is around us. If we ask questions, we don't want to wait for the answers. We want immediate results.

In Psalms 46, God is commanding us to put a pause on our busy lifestyles and constant questioning, and for one moment simply still our hearts and realize who He is. Doing this is something that is crucial to handing over the entire puzzle to God, every piece, every ounce of strength used to try and figure it out, every doubt, every fear, and every hope. We really must take Psalms 46:10 to heart when it tells us to "be still." But that is not all that it tells us. It tells us to "know that I am God." I like how this verse is translated in *The Message:* "Step out of the traffic! Take a long, loving look at Me, your High God, above politics, above everything." Before we take any other step in giving our whole entire puzzle to God, no matter how much in a hurry we are to put things together or have God make sense of it all, we just have to *be still* and simply marvel in the fact that He is God! How often do we take just five minutes to quiet our hearts, step out of our surroundings, get away from the noise and apprehension and become totally in awe of who God is and what He wants to do for us? I don't do it near as often as I should. But when we take the time to really "be still" and recognize God's power and authority, an amazing peace will override all worry, all fear, and all doubt.

Look back at the story of Peter. When Peter saw Jesus walking on the water he first thought Jesus was a ghost. Then Jesus called out to Peter, just as two best friends would say to each other "It's me," so that Peter would recognize His voice. Before Peter jumped out of the boat to walk on water, amidst a raging storm and crashing waves, he simply had to be still for one second and know that it was Jesus' voice he heard calling out to him from across the waves. However, Peter didn't trust for sure that it was Jesus and so he decided to test the voice calling out to him, by seeing if he could walk on top of the water, something only Jesus could allow him to do.

How many times in life do we act as Peter and amidst all of the hustle and bustle of life, the storms and the valleys, doubt that God is calling us to come into the unknown and simply let *Him* guide us there? If only we would for one moment *be still* and rest assured that God is God and He *is* calling for us to come and follow Him into His plan for our lives. I think that so many times we just get so caught up in the craziness of life that we forget to step back and recognize God's absolute power, His wondrous works, and His complete sovereignty over the entire universe. If we took the time to do this more often, we'd slowly begin to realize to Whom we're giving our lives – present and future – over to: the God of the Universe, the God above all gods, the Creator of all things. This fact alone should immediately cause us to never doubt God or want control again, but possessing our natural human nature, unfortunately it's often not that easy for us. That is where trust comes into play—letting down all hope that trust and dependence in the flesh is enough, and gaining the wisdom that complete trust in God is the only way that is going to get us through the mysteries of our life that cause pain, wonder, anger, and sadness. Trust is the second step to letting go of the puzzle and handing it over to God.

– – –

It's sad to say but we're living in a world of lies, deceit, and disappointment. Many of us have experienced times of sorrow after sorrow and we have gotten to the point where the trust that anything good will happen at all has gone out the window and we simply don't want to trust in anything, or any*one* for that matter. Perhaps you've been lied to your whole life by someone and when you finally found out the truth it left you in a place where trusting anyone around you was almost impossible. Maybe you know someone who has countless times broken his or her promises to you. Trusting others is something that does not come easy to people that have gone through these experiences.

Others of us haven't completely stopped trusting, but we've turned over to trusting in our own flesh, believing that trust and security in our own flesh is enough to get us by. But there's one thing that I know for sure: Trusting in human flesh, or anything else besides God, is a whole different experience from trusting in the Almighty God Himself.

Trusting in people, ourselves included (flesh) or anything else (money, possessions, grades) has its risks. Of course, I know that there are some people in my life that I can trust. I can trust my parents to provide for me—food, clothing, and shelter. I can trust my best friend to keep her promises to me and to keep my secrets safe. I trust in these people – my parents, friends, my youth sponsors – but I have to realize that these same people *are* capable of breaking promises and letting me down. I have to realize that no human is perfect and mistakes are going to be made. Dates are going to be forgotten. Secrets are going to occasionally slip out. And although it doesn't happen often, I still have to remember that no human being on earth will never let me down.

That's where the difference comes in. Trusting in God has zero risks. He will never break a promise to us, He will never forget to show up, and He will never take us down into the valley of sadness without personally escorting us back up onto the mountaintop of hope and deliverance. If we want to hand all the pieces of the puzzle over to God it is crucial that we develop this total trust in God—and in nothing and no one else.

Proverbs 3:5 in the NIV says, "Trust in God with all your heart and lean not on your own understanding..." The *Message* says it like this: "Trust God from the bottom of your heart; don't try to figure out everything on your own." When we "lean on our own understanding" it gets us nowhere because we simply can't understand the way the pieces go together and we can't see the big picture. When certain things happen in our lives it's going to seem as though God doesn't know what He's doing and we may even feel as if He has betrayed us at some point. But I promise you, when you trust in God with all of your heart, you can rest assured that He is doing what He believes is best for you, even if it means going through a time of confusing sorrow or complete loneliness. Believe in your heart that God is not going to leave you in those valleys! He has plans to give you a "future and a hope," remember?

Trusting that God has us right where He wants us to be in order to accomplish His plan for our lives is one of the biggest steps we can take as Christians. Trusting God every single hour of the day helps us to develop a lifetime dependence on His provision and His will–through the good times and the bad. Trusting in God means, instead of questioning God's ways and worrying that He's lost control, takinge a pure delight in every situation in life with a calming peace that puts our hearts at rest. It means using the hard times in life as opportunities to grow closer to God and develop a deeper relationship with Him.

James 5:1-4 says this: "Consider it pure joy, my brothers, whenever you face trials of many kinds, because you know that the testing of your faith develops perseverance. Perseverance must finish its work so that you may be mature and complete, not lacking anything." (NIV)

My very best friend, Jillian, was recently going through a very hard time in her life. All around the same time she broke up with her boyfriend and lost a relationship with one of her very best friends after her friend had stabbed her in the back. God's very best seemed to her like the very worst, but fortunately she was able to recognize that those hard times were times that she could draw closer to her Savior, times that she could "develop perseverance." One time I asked her to brainstorm some ideas for this book before I had begun it and it hadn't been too long after she had gone through those awful times. One of her brainstorming ideas was to talk about hard times in life and this is what she wrote about them:

"Sometimes the hard times that come our way are totally out of our control. It is during these times when it becomes very easy to blame God for the hard things we are facing, [the things] that we did nothing to deserve. However, these are the times that we need to draw even closer into the arms of our loving Father. I have found that during these times of heartache there can also be an amazing time of spiritual growth, because we learn to depend on God more and more. We must always rest in the fact that God is always faithful. He never promised a hardship-free life, but He did always promise to be with us each step of the way."

What an awesome trust those words display, and how awesome it would be if this generation began to develop the same trust in God with every circumstance, every piece of the puzzle. Why? I'll tell you why. Because after we take the time to be still and realize Who God is and develop an unshakable trust in Him, we can tear down the veil of fear and apprehension and surrender every passion, every goal, and every dream to God.

— — —

When God made us He put inside of us unique talents, abilities, and skills. He gave us different passions and aspirations for our futures. For example: I absolutely love to dance, especially hip-hop. When I can shut my door in my room, turn the music up loud and just let loose–that's when I feel the most alive. When I learn a hip-hop dance, I like to perform it over and over and perfect the moves, and even when I do finally get it right, I have such a fun time doing it that I just keep practicing it. Dancing is most definitely one of my God-given passions.

A HOPE AND A FUTURE: LEARNING TO TRUST GOD WITH THE PUZZLE OF LIFE

For others among you, maybe you have a passion for singing or playing a musical instrument. Maybe you come alive when you're playing a certain sport or when you're out there just helping others. If you can't think of one, ask yourself this: *What am I doing when I become totally alive? What is it that makes me forget about everything else in life, if only for a moment, and just think about this one thing that I'm doing?* Maybe God has given you more than one passion, but whether He's given you a single one that you can point out for sure or if He's given you three different passions, He's placed them inside of you for a reason and He wants you to use those passions to bring glory to Him.

After we have developed the amazing trust in God that I mentioned earlier, we *have* to surrender these passions, along with all of our goals and dreams, over to God if we wish for Him to take over putting our puzzle together. When we try and hang on to any part of them, our flesh instantly rises up and begins to tell us that (for some reason) we own these things, that we have the right to decide how they're handled. That very thought is so far from the truth—we do not in reality have any right at all to hang on to the dreams and passions that God has given us. Besides, if we can't see the big picture, how do we know the best way to use them and which way to go with our dreams? The only very right way to discover a passion, to envision a dream, and to set a goal, is to immediately give it back to God and allow Him to work out all of the details that go along with it, whether it means shaping your circumstances to allow that dream to come true or that passion to be used in a certain way, or reshaping your heart's desires to coincide with His will, perhaps being a different dream that He wants you to follow.

Worrying about the future, giving God my dreams and passions, and trusting that He's going to give me His very best has been somewhat of a challenge to me. It seems that every other month I have a new idea of what I want to do after high school or what I want to do for my career. *Which passion do I want to follow in a career? How long do I want to go into mission training after high school before I go on to college? Which major do I choose in college?* At one point this year I had my mind totally made up. I was going to go to the same missions training school that my sister had gone to, only in a different state, for about five months the fall after high school. Next I would go on to a specific college in Indiana, major in youth ministry, marry a youth pastor, and live happily ever after. I thought it was the perfect plan for the next six or seven years of my life and I was glad that I finally had a "structured" future ahead of me.

Just this past summer when my youth group went to Columbus, which I shared a little bit about in Chapter Five, the theme for the week was "Big God, Big Dreams." I won't discuss every single thing we talked about that week, but to say the least, by the end of the trip I came to realize that – guess what Tessa? – God gave you dreams, He gave you passions, and He's *going* to give you a future, but you've got to lay it all down and quit "scheduling" your future, when you should be taking it one day at a time, handing every single hour over to God. I'm reminded of some verses in James: "Now listen, you who say, 'Today or tomorrow we will go to this or that city, spend a year there, carry on business and make money.' Why, you do not even know what will happen tomorrow. What is your life? You are a mist that appears for a little while and then vanishes. Instead, you ought to say, 'If it is the Lord's will, we will live and do this or that'." (James 4:13-15, NIV)

It's true. My life is only a swift vapor that passes in and out of this world before I can count to ten. I could die in five years, I could die in five months, or I could die tomorrow.

Only God knows the day that I'll finally get to see His face in Heaven. And since I do not know the day I do not have the right to plan out my future without giving it all to God and letting Him put it all together. Tomorrow has not yet arrived, but only today. *Today* we must give our dreams to God. *Today* we must give our fears to God. *Today* we must give God our passions and goals. *Today* we have to trust that God has our every triumph, our every success, our every moment of sorrow, our every confusion, our every tear of joy, and our every tear of sadness *in His hands*.

God is the giver of all dreams and He wants us to dream big, because, as Philippians 4:13 says, "I can do everything through him who gives me strength." (NIV) With God, we can accomplish anything in the entire world through us—but we must seek out His will and hand every detail over to Him before we do anything else. God has His very best in mind for us and whether that means going through good times or bad times, if we keep our mind on giving God every moment, triumph will be ours.

– – –

Don't Forget This
Key points on the future

- We were meant to live lives of passion and purpose.
- God has a future of hope and purpose planned for every single person.
- No matter how hard we try to fit together the pieces of the puzzle, we'll never be able to do it; only God can see the big picture.
- Our focus has to be kept away from the "waves" of life and directly on Christ.

- We cannot put any of our confidence in our own flesh to get through but our trust must be completely in God alone.
- Jesus is calling us into the unknown and in order to answer His call we have to 1) be still and *know* He is God, 2) totally trust Him with everything, even the hard times that seem to overcome us, and 3) surrender our passions, dreams, goals, and even our fears over to God and let Him direct our path daily.
- God wants us to dream big.

Before you ask God to give you something tomorrow, make sure that you've given Him everything today.

— — —

My Thoughts

_____

_____

_____

_____

_____

_____

— — —

Chapter 10

Finishing The Race: Keeping The Bar Raised And The Passion Strong

Philippians 3:12-16, "I'm not saying that I have this all together, that I have it made. But I am well on my way, reaching out for Christ, who has so wondrously reached out for me. Friends, don't get me wrong: By no means do I count myself an expert in all of this, but I've got my eye on the goal, where God is beckoning us onward—to Jesus. I'm off and running, and I'm not turning back. So let's keep focused on that goal, those of us who want everything God has for us. If any of you have something else in mind, something less than total commitment, God will clear your blurred vision—you'll see it yet! Now that we're on the right track, let's stay on it." (Msg)

It happens to me all too easily. It happens two days after I hear a really awesome sermon. It happens a week after I get home from a powerful mission trip or a "life-changing" week at church camp. It happens two weeks after I read a book that inspires me, motivates me, and challenges me to go deeper into my walk with God. I lose track. I forget what I heard, what I did, or what I read. The ignited passion to change my life quietly, slowly, and ever so slyly begins to fade away and I go back to living my "normal life"—the life I lived before that "life-changing" moment, the life that is routine, the life that is average, and the life that only days before I thought I had given up on.

A few weeks ago I had the opportunity to go on a weekend retreat out in Colorado with the authors of my favorite books and twelve other young women from all over the country. It was one of the most amazing weekends I've ever experienced. It *was* life changing for me and on the plane ride home I felt as though I was a new person—with a deeper passion for God, a new attitude on life, and a changed heart. The day after I got home was the first day back at school. How's that for a "welcome back to the real world" slap in the face? When I woke up for the first day of school it hadn't even been twenty-four hours since I had returned home to the "real world." Let's just say that Satan had no luck attacking me that day and I still felt a changed girl inside of me—a girl of more joy, more peace, and more patience. As the days went on and my life became an early morning to late at night routine I felt more and more pressure to slip back into the life I knew before—the mediocre Christian life of a person that loves God and has her occasional "God moments" where God does something radical in her heart, whispers a brand new truth in her mind, or brings about a temporary lifestyle change. It was incredibly hard to remember the things I learned and to put them into practice because the life that I came home wanting to live was seen in almost no one around me. But I told myself: *Tessa, you are not going to let this life-changing experience slip away from you this time! God has spoken so much truth to you in just the past week and to let it go and only remember it for a few days would be a total waste. You have to remember it! You have to live it! Keep pressing on towards that goal, Tessa.* I wanted more than anything to be back in Colorado surrounded by other young women that shared my desires and were cheering me on towards greatness in my relationship with Christ, but I knew that was obviously impossible and that no matter how hard I tried, I had to go back into the "real world" and live out that changed life no matter how challenging it would be. It was very demanding of me yet I wanted it badly enough.

I know there are many of you out there that have had experiences like I had. Maybe it was when you first became a Christian. You felt excited, changed, and ready to go all out for God. Maybe it was after your youth group went to a Christian convention or on a mission trip and while you were there you totally felt the presence of God working in your life. For those of you that like to read a lot like me, it could have been after you read a certain book that inspired you and motivated you. That also has happened a lot to me. God has delivered a new truth into my life through something I read and I get excited and ready to hang on to that truth and live it out, only to forget what I read and how God had spoken to me a few days, weeks, or months later.

As I'm writing this, I'm thinking, *How many people are going to read this book and go through the "summer camp" experience? How many people will read this book, and hearing God speak to them, be encouraged to change a certain area in their life, make some changes, and then forget about it all the week after?* My hope is that it would be no one and that is why I want to end with a final encouragement to raise the bar…and keep it raised.

First off, take some time to think about how has God spoken to you lately, whether it's been while you were reading this book or not. What truths has He been gently whispering into your ear? Write down at least two:

_____

_____

_____

_____

_____

Now ask yourself this: Who or what in your life is Satan going to try and use to cause these truths to fade away and cause you to lose your fire and passion for the very truth and word of God?

_____

_____

_____

_____

_____

_____

_____

If any of you are truly interested in changing the way you live your life, going deeper with God, abandoning the world and running away with God's truth while transforming your generation in the meantime, it's going to take a lot of commitment. It's also going to take the willingness to make painful or difficult choices in your life that God is calling you to make. No one ever said that living a life surrendered to God was painless and undemanding. God never promised us an effortless and trouble-free existence, but He did promise to be with us every step of the way and bring us a victory that nothing else could bring.

Raising the bar in this generation by living this life that God has called us to is one of those things that could easily bring about temporary excitement and lifestyle changes along with short-lived "spiritual highs" among us if we don't take the time to really change from the inside out, commit to what we're doing, and surrender it all back to the very hand of God. In order to make a lasting and permanent change within ourselves and within the world around us, there are several things we must do, things that will help us to stay passionate about making a difference and things that will help us develop a deeper relationship with God along the way.

— — —

Fellowship and Accountability

Hebrews 10:24-25, "Let's see how inventive we can be in encouraging love and helping out, not avoiding worshiping together as some do but spurring each other on, especially as we see the big day approaching." (Msg)

We were never meant to live out our Christian lives without the support of people around us. We need encouragement from people to lift us up and tell us to keep going when the times get hard and we feel weak in our relationship with God. We need to know others are running the race right along with us and are headed towards the same prize. That is why it is so incredibly important that we take the time to develop solid friendships with other Christian young women that desire to live a life completely devoted to God. Engaging in fellowship with other believers allows us to develop a support group in which we can practice keeping each other *accountable*.

Keeping one another accountable is so crucial to staying on track, yet it seems to be so rare among us. We're afraid to offend someone by keeping them accountable or we get offended ourselves when someone gently rebukes us. But the type of accountability that God wants us to give and receive is one that is based on sincere love and humility that comes from God alone.

Too often our human nature kicks in and when we go through a spiritual transformation and begin to grow in Christ the thought forms in our head that it's our own doing, which results in a prideful heart that has a hard time accepting loving admonitions from other Christians. Furthermore, when someone *else* goes through a spiritual transformation, it is common for our flesh to rise to the surface and instead of cheering such persons on and desiring to see them succeed and grow stronger, we carefully watch out for them to sin, so that the very instant we see them make a mistake we can say, "Ha! I knew it wouldn't last" or "Thank goodness I'm doing so much better than she is." As girls I think we have a tendency to be very quick to compare ourselves with other girls and we form a competitive spirit that results in critical minds, gossiping mouths, and judgmental hearts.

It's very easy for us to look around and "evaluate" our "spirituality" with those around us and think, "Well, as long as I'm doing better than her, I'm doing good enough." As a result we keep on the lookout for that "her" to stumble into sin so that we can give ourselves more "spiritual points" because we think we're that much ahead.

Our relationship with God is not a competition. It's not a race to see who sins the most on the weekend, who reads their Bible the most, or who prays the best. It's about constantly determining where *we* are in our *own* relationship with God and doing whatever we can daily to grow stronger, becoming more mature in Christ and imitating His nature.

Accountability is not something that brings condemnation. It's not an excuse to say, "I told you so." Accountability comes from a genuine love for others and a desire to spur them on to a more intimate and meaningful relationship with Christ.

Galatians 6:1 says, "Brothers, if someone is caught in sin, you who are spiritual should restore him gently. But watch yourself, or you also may be tempted." (NIV) We are to take on the responsibility of keeping our sisters in Christ accountable, but we must be able to take it from others as well. It is a good idea to find an "accountability" partner, a person that you trust desires to see you grow closer to Christ and surrender everything to His will. An accountability partner is someone that would also desire for you to keep them accountable in their relationship with God. It doesn't even have to be a relationship with only one other person but it can also be a small group of people that all desire to lift each other up, gently and humbly. Whether you have one or numerous accountability partners , always make sure that the relationships are based on love and not competition and pride and always keep Christ the center of the friendship, because without Him, the purpose is only defeated.

— — —

CONFESSIONS OF A GIRL

My Thoughts

Is there someone you know that you'd like to keep you accountable? Who is this person? What do you see in them that makes you desire a friendship? Sincerity? Love for others? Is there someone in your life that you have been in a "spiritual competition" with? What do you need to do to change that relationship?

FINISHING THE RACE: KEEPING THE BAR RAISED AND THE PASSION STRONG

PRAYING FOR OUR GENERATION

1 Thessalonians 5:17, "Pray continually." (NIV)

I believe that the power of prayer has been widely underestimated and that the very idea of prayer has become distorted. To so many the idea of praying means saying a little prayer for five minutes in the morning or taking a few moments to say "bedtime prayers." Prayer is something that the Bible tells us to do continually, all the time, constantly, throughout the day. It is not something that requires us to think of the best words we can so that we sound as "holy" as we can, but praying *"continually"* simply requires us to keep a prayerful mind that at any moment can step aside and offer a whispered request to God, a shout of gratitude, or just a simple "I *love* You, God! You are so amazing to me!"

Of course there are times that we need to set aside during the day to specifically spend with God, praying to Him, listening to His voice, and seeking His will. But we don't have to limit ourselves to praying only when we're by ourselves in our room or when we sit down to a meal. Prayer is something that can dwell in our minds through every moment of the day if we train ourselves to constantly keep our thoughts turned towards God.

Prayer is a very powerful tool and we need to start using it. If we dedicate ourselves to praying "continually" for our generation, I can promise you that God will begin to do amazing things that we never thought possible. God can soften any heart, even if it seems to be as hard as stone. God can heal any pain and remove any hurt, no matter how deeply it is rooted. I wonder what would happen if we really began to pray more for our generation and more specifically, for those around us that we see on a daily basis, even if we only know them by name?

I've often thought to myself, *How on earth can my little prayers affect a hardened heart let alone an entire generation?* But that's just it! It isn't *me* doing the work in others, but it's *God* doing the work through His own power. And that is why prayer is so effective–it's not the power of the person praying, but the power of the Person they're praying to. My heart's desire is that we would begin to unleash this power within us (Jesus) and use it to change the lives of those around us and to display the power and glory of God and Who He is and everything that He has done for us. If we do, the possibilities are endless.

Let God begin to develop in you a prayerful heart that is constantly giving Him praise and thanksgiving and a heart that is lovingly praying for your world. In the process, you will grow into a deeper relationship with God and at the same time you will be discovering one of the most powerful tools that God gave us.

My Thoughts
Is there someone in your life that God laid on your heart to pray for? What would you like to see God do in their life? What specific issue(s) that our generation is dealing with has God given you a passion to pray for? How would you like to see God work?

_____

_____

_____

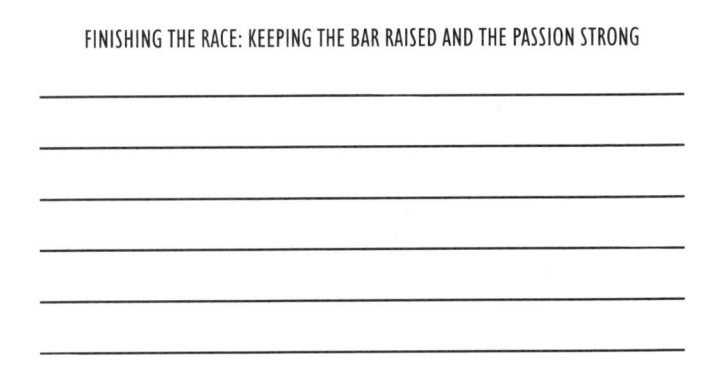

Let it be Known and Remembered

Psalms 40:9-10, "I've preached you to the whole congregation, I've kept back nothing, God—you know that. I didn't keep the news of your ways a secret, didn't keep it to myself. I told it all, how dependable you are, how thorough. I didn't hold back pieces of love and truth for myself alone. I told it all, let the congregation know the whole story." (Msg)

This past Christmas season my family and I experienced a true miracle. God restored a portion of my hearing that was never supposed to come back. It was an enormous answer to the prayers that so many people around me had been praying for me for months. I'm not going into details about it but I'll say that the power of God was wonderfully displayed that Christmas season and it was an amazing experience for me. When I first noticed that I could hear better, I wanted to tell everyone around me—I was totally overjoyed and couldn't wait to tell people how God had answered a prayer.

As the months went on, the miracle was still something very dear to me but I slowly began to categorize it as "old news" and was more hesitant to go into detail about the whole story when I told people about it. Sometimes I was even tempted to think to myself, *Well, God didn't restore* all *of my hearing to me...* I began to undermine the hugeness of what God had done in my life through the whole experience.

One day my mom came to me and told me that our pastor had asked her if we would speak of the miracle for a few minutes in church one Sunday so that the whole congregation could give God glory for the awesome thing that He had done.

"But everyone already knows," was my first response. We had already told so many people and there had even been a little write-up about it in the youth group newsletter.

"Tessa, there are people out there that don't know and we need to make this awesome work known. We *cannot* forget what God has done."

The last, but definitely not least, thing I want to encourage you to do to "keep the bar raised" is to *tell someone* what God has done for you. Has He brought you to Him for the first time? Has He given you a new insight on something? Has He challenged you to a closer walk with Him? Don't keep it in. Don't hold it in as a secret. When God does something in your life, it's tempting to be excited about it at first and tell the people around us about it, but it's all too easy to slowly let it die down and forget about it.

When God does something in your life—let it be known! Tell others what God has done in your life. Tell them what He has spoken to you. Tell them how He has changed your life. We'll never be able to know how we impact people just by our words. You'll never be able to tell just how many people were changed by something you said. God's goodness displayed on earth is something worthy of shouting to the world! We need to celebrate the things that God does for us and make sure that we don't hold on to them for just some time, but that we're always mindful of them and that we're always thanking God for them. They don't have to be just physical healings or big "spiritual breakthroughs" but they can be times when God has healed you spiritually or emotionally or simply times that He has spoken a new truth into your life through His word or through someone else.

If we want our generation to change, we have to tell it how *we* have been changed and what an impact God's truth has had on our lives. Curiosity will spark. People will begin to wonder. Questions will be asked. The mystery will be revealed.

– – –

My Thoughts
What has God done for you or spoken to you that you need to tell others about? What's holding you back? Embarrassment? Fear of rejection? What are some other things you can do to never forget the things that God does for you?

_____

_____

_____

_____

_____

_____

_____

– – –

Matthew 7:13-14, "Enter through the narrow gate. For wide is the gate and broad is the road that leads to destruction, and many enter through it. But small is the gate and narrow the road that leads to life, and only a few find it." (NIV)

And this is what I have to share. These are the words in my heart. This is what God has spoken to me and this is the life I desire to live. A life of surrender. A life of fulfillment in God. A life of pure desire to bring glory to Him in everything that I do and say. As I'm entering through the narrow gate, will you join me? God is waiting on the other side, and He is so passionately cheering us on—cheering us on to a life of love, a life of passion and joy, and a life that you will never want to turn away from. This is my confession to the rest of my generation. Take the truth—and run with it.

Pray for a Cure

Before her junior year, Tessa was diagnosed with Neurofibromatosis 2, a genetic disorder affecting the auditory nerves. Hearing loss beginning in the teens or early twenties is generally the first symptom. The Childrens Tumor Foundation is an organization dedicated to ending Neurofibromatisis through research. For more information about their research, visit http://www.ctf.org.

ALSO FROM FRESH WRITERS BOOKS

Fax Orders: (707)-220-4510. Send this form. E-Mail Orders: store@MrExcel.com
Online: http://www.FreshWritersBooks.com
Postal Orders: Fresh Writers, 13386 Judy Ave NW, Uniontown OH 44685, USA

Title	Quantity	Price	Total
Confessions of a Girl – Truth to be Told By Tessa Sean Hershberger (ISBN 1-932902-97-5) 222 pages An inspiring and motivational book for all young women and girls, Tessa shares her deepest thoughts and insights with the rest of her generation. An honest and truthful look into what every girl is secretly longing for deep down inside.		$7.95	
The Heart's Flames By Ashley Shawntel (ISBN 1-932802-99-1) 163 pages A Christian romance novel finds Arizona smoke jumper Cole Hunter must deal with the loss of his best friend and his hearing. While being treated for hearing loss, his wife Julie is involved in an affair at their church. Can Cole have the strength to repair all?		$5.95	
A World of Difference By Lee Galada (ISBN 1-932802-98-3) 154 pages A Sci-Fi thriller set on Mars in 2350. Humans have colonized Mars and the world is living in peace, until Earth mounts a secret military to invade. Can young Darren McAndrews and his teammates halt the invasion?		$5.95	
Baker's Dozen By Joshua Matthew Moorhead (ISBN 1-932802-96-7) 217 pages Discover the impact of 9/11 on a generation. This is 13 days in the life of Justin Baker, a high school senior who is living the best of times in the summer of 2001. Justin's journal moves fast– from scandals on the faculty to covert ops on the school roof, from history class to history itself. In just 13 days, Justin and the world will change.		$9.95	

Name: _____

Address: _____

City, State, Zip: _____

E-Mail: _____

        Sales Tax: Ohio residents add 6.5% sales tax
Shipping by Air: US $4 for first book, $2 per additional book.
  International: $9 for first book, $5 per additional book.

Payment: Check or Money order to "Tickling Keys, Inc." or pay with VISA/MC/American Express:

Card #:_____ Exp.:_____

Name on Card: _____

Bulk Orders: Ordering enough for the entire youth group? Save 40% when you order 6 or more of any one title.